A
Liturgical
Psalter
for the
Christian
Year

Prepared and Edited by

Massey H. Shepherd Jr.

With the Assistance of the
Consultation on Common Texts

1976
Augsburg Publishing House • Minneapolis
The Liturgical Press • Collegeville

Copyright © 1976 Massey H. Shepherd Jr.

Library of Congress Catalog Card No. 76-21464

International Standard Book No. 0-8066-1545-1

Published by
Augsburg Publishing House
Minneapolis, Minnesota
        and
The Liturgical Press
Collegeville, Minnesota

Manufactured in the United States of America

CONTENTS

* Psalms with Hallelujah

FOREWORD

The Psalms of the Old Testament have a large place in the worship and devotions of Christians. Whether in whole or in part, or in hymns and prayers inspired by them, they have made a lasting impress upon our praise and prayer. This is not surprising. They were the hymnbook and prayer book of Jesus and his early disciples, who considered them prophetic of our Lord's life and mission. The Psalter is one of the most frequently quoted books in the New Testament. The prophetic interpretation of the psalms in the writings of the New Testament and the early Church Fathers provides the clue to their use in the liturgy of the church.

This selection is based upon those psalms that came to be associated in the church's historic liturgies with the principal seasons and holy days of the Christian year, in commemoration of the redemptive work of Christ and the life of his church. Certain psalms have been included which have found a common, general use on Sundays and weekdays. The appended "Notes on the Psalms" provide information about their history, meaning, and liturgical use.

The following collection is designed primarily, though not exclusively, for use at the Eucharist, in the places traditionally assigned to psalmody in the rite. The translations are based upon the original Hebrew text. Where this is obscure, or where there is a choice of readings of it, we have selected a rendering more appropriate to the needs of Christian worshipers. In some cases readings have been taken from the ancient Greek and Latin versions, since these have been official Psalters of the church through many centuries. Verses of imprecation have been omitted, for they are unsuitable to wor-

5

ship at the Eucharist; but there is no elimination of themes of judgment. Some acclamations and refrains have been supplied where these seem to be justified by the ancient texts.

Two features of this translation should be noted. First, we have favored the use of LORD, customary in many English versions, in place of the Hebrew name *Yahweh* that is now finding its way into many contemporary translations of the Bible, for the reasons stated in the preface of the Common Bible, an ecumenical edition of the Revised Standard Version (Cleveland: Collins, 1973). Second, for the Hebrew word *hesed,* which the Revised Standard Version consistently translates as "steadfast love," we have employed various renderings found in English versions of the Bible, depending upon the context and the rhythm of the verses, such as: love, mercy, goodness, loving-kindness. This is a rich word in Hebrew that cannot be comprehended by any word in English; for it refers to God's faithful and unfailing love and favor to his people.

Special attention has been given to the poetic arrangement of the psalms by verses and strophes (stanzas). With each psalm one or more antiphons are suggested, where these are desired for use; but the listing is by no means exhaustive of the rich treasure of texts in both the Old and the New Testaments. Antiphons help to give thematic emphasis to a psalm in major seasons or on special holy days. The "Notes on Liturgical Use" provide ways of reciting or singing the psalms effectively. These may be in unison or by alternate or antiphonal groups. Where musical resources are available, soloists, choirs, and congregation may render them in varied combinations of alternating song. The texts lend themselves to musical composition in either chant form—unison or harmonized—or choral anthems, with possibilities of combining the two methods of singing.

The Consultation on Common Texts offers this Psalter with no desire to compete with the versions authorized in the several churches, but with the hope that its use, ecumenically shared, may contribute to that unity among Christians one with another for whom our Lord prayed "that they may all be one."

VERSES AND STROPHES

The verses are enumerated according to the Common Bible. In this translation some verses are divided into two parts for purposes of rendition, in which case, for ease of reference, an additional verse number is provided: e.g., *[5a], [17a].*

Each verse of a psalm has two or three lines, commonly known as stichs. These may be referred to as 1*a*, 1*b*, 1*c*.

Strophes or stanzas are noted by the letters *A, B, C, D,* etc. Certain psalms have major divisions noted by captions in Roman numerals (I, II, etc.). Many of these are psalms of composite origin.

ANTIPHONS

Antiphons are thematic verses taken from the Psalms or other passages of the Scriptures. They may be said or sung before and after a psalm, or, where desired, between each verse or group of verses also. They do not replace the Gloria Patri, a Christian doxology which from ancient times has been added at the end of every psalm or portion of a psalm in Christian worship. The text of the Gloria Patri recommended by the ecumenical International Consultation on English Texts is this:

Glory to the Father, and to the Son, and to the Holy Spirit:
as it was in the beginning, is now, and will be for ever. Amen.

ALLELUIA

Certain psalms with an asterisk in the table of contents have *Hallelujah* ("Praise the LORD") sometimes at the beginning and the end. If preferred, the Greek form *Alleluia* may be used. This acclamation, according to ancient custom, is omitted in the season of Lent. In these psalms it may be used as the antiphon.

THE PSALMS

Psalm 1

A 1   Blessed are they
         who do not follow the advice of the wicked,
         nor take their stance in the way of sinners,
         nor seat themselves in company with the scoffers.

    2   Their delight is in the law of the Lord,
         and in his law they meditate day and night.

    3   They are like a tree planted by water-brooks,
            that bears its fruit in season,
            with leaves that never wither.
         In everything they do, they prosper.

B 4   Not so with the wicked!
         They are like chaff blown away by the wind;
    5   they will not rise up in the Judgment,
         nor will sinners in the company of the just.

    6   For the Lord knows the way of the just;
         but the way of the wicked will perish.

ANTIPHONS

Prov. 2:8:
The Lord guards the paths of justice,
   and preserves the way of his saints.

Jer. 17:7-8:
Blessed are they who trust in the Lord;
   they are like a tree that never ceases to bear fruit.

Matt. 7:17, 20:
A sound tree bears good fruit, a bad tree evil fruit;
   by their fruits you will know them.

John 14:6:
I am the way and the truth and the life;
   no one comes to the Father but by me.

Rev. 2:7:
The victors shall eat from the tree of life,
   that stands in the paradise of God.

A 1   Why are the nations in an uproar,
         and the peoples muttering empty threats?
   2   The kings of the earth rise up in revolt,
         and rulers plot against the LORD and his Anointed:

   3   "Let us break out of their yoke,
             and fling off their bonds from us!"

B 4   The LORD laughs at them from his throne in heaven;
         he mocks them in his scorn.
   5   Then he speaks to them in his fury;
         and his rage strikes terror in them:

   6   "I myself have established my King
             upon Zion, my holy mountain."

C 7   I will tell you the LORD's decree for me:

            "You are my Son; today I have begotten you.
   8   Ask of me: I give you the nations for your heritage,
             and the ends of the earth for your possession.
   9   You will crush them with a rod of iron,
             and shatter them like pieces of pottery."

D 10   Therefore, be wary, you kings;
         take warning, you rulers of the earth:

   11   "Serve the LORD with fear,
             and with trembling kiss his feet
   12   lest he be angry and you perish,
             for his wrath is quickly kindled."

ANTIPHONS

Verse 7: Easter, Epiphany, or Transfiguration.

Ps. 103:19:

The LORD has set his throne in heaven,
   and his kingdom rules over all.

Isa. 60:3:

The nations shall come to your light,
   and kings to the brightness of your rising.

Rev. 15:4:

All nations shall come and worship you,
   for your judgments have been revealed.

11

Psalm 8

     1   O LORD, our Lord,
         how glorious is your Name in all creation!

A   2   Your majesty is praised above the heavens;
         it is sung below by babes and little children.
     3   You have founded a stronghold against your foes,
         to silence your enemies and avengers.

B   4   When I look up to your sky, the work of your fingers,
         the moon and the stars that you set in their courses,
     5   What is man that you should be mindful of him,
         or the son of man that you should care for him?

C   6   Yet you made him in the image of yourself,
         and crowned him with glory and honor.
     7   You gave him rule over your handiwork,
         and put all things under his dominion:

D   8   All sheep and cattle,
         and also the wild animals;
     9   Birds of the air, fish of the sea,
         and whatever makes its path through the waters.

    10   O LORD, our Lord,
         how glorious is your Name in all creation!

ANTIPHONS

Verses 1 and 10: General.

Gen. 1:26:

Let us make man in our image and likeness,
    and let them have dominion over the earth and the sea.

Rev. 4:11:

You are worthy, our God,
    to receive glory and honor and power;
For you created all things,
    and by your will they exist and are created.

1   LORD, who may lodge in your tent,
        or make a home on your holy mountain?

A   2   "He who lives blamelessly, doing what is right,
        and who speaks the truth from his heart.
    3   His tongue is not used for malice;
        he never wrongs his friend,
        nor casts any slurs on his neighbor.

B   4   He looks with disdain on the evil-minded,
        but honors those who revere the LORD.
    5   If he swears to his hurt, he does not retract;
        nor does he lend his money for gain,
        or take a bribe against the innocent."

6   Whoever does these things
        will stand firm for ever.

ANTIPHONS

John 15:14:
You are my friends,
    if you do what I command you.

James 1:22:
Be doers of the word,
    and not hearers only.

I

A   1   The heavens declare the glory of God;
             the vault of the sky shows his handiwork.
      2   Day after day tells it out,
             and night after night makes it known.
      3   There are no words, no language,
             nor voices that are heard.
      4   Yet their sound has gone out to all lands,
             and their words to the end of the world.

B   5   In the sea he pitched a tent for the sun,
             who comes out from his canopy as a bridegroom,
             and rejoices as a champion in a race.
      6   He rises from one edge of the heavens,
             and makes his circuit to the other;
             and nothing is hidden from his heat.

II

C   7   The law of the Lord is perfect,
                   and renews life.
         The decrees of the Lord are trustworthy,
                   and make wise the simple.
      8   The statutes of the Lord are just,
                   and rejoice the heart.
         The commands of the Lord are clear,
                   and enlighten the eyes.
      9   The fear of the Lord is holy,
                   and endures for ever.
         The judgments of the Lord are true,
                   and altogether right.

     10   They are more desirable than gold,
                   more than the purest gold.
         Sweeter are they than honey,
                   than honey from the comb.

D 11 By your law your servant is taught;
  and in keeping it there is great reward.

12 Who can discern his faults?—
  Of those I am not aware, forgive me.

13 Keep your servant away from the insolent,
  lest they get the better of me.

[13a] Then shall I be blameless,
  and innocent of grievous offense.

14 Let the words of my mouth,
   and the thoughts of my heart,
  Find favor in your sight,
   O LORD, my rock and my redeemer.

ANTIPHONS

Verse 1: Trinity Sunday; General.

Verse 4: Saints' Days: apostles and missionaries.

Verse 5: Christmas; Epiphany.

Verse 14: Saints' Days; General.

Isa. 45:8: Christmas or Epiphany

Drop down the dew from above, O heavens,
 and let the clouds rain justice.
Let the earth's womb be opened
 and bring forth a Savior.

I

A 1 My God, my God, why have you forsaken me?
    Why are you so far from helping me,
    and from the cry of my distress?
  2 My God, I cry to you in the daytime,
    but you do not answer;
    and in the night also, but I find no rest.

  3 Yet you are the Holy One,
    enthroned above the praises of Israel.
  4 Our fathers put their trust in you;
    they trusted you, and you delivered them.
  5 When they cried to you, you set them free;
    they trusted you and were not put to shame.

  6 As for me, I am a worm and hardly a man,
    scorned by everyone and despised by the people.
  7 All who see me deride me and make sport of me,
    curling their lips and tossing their heads:
  8 "He trusted in the LORD; let him save him!
    let him rescue him if he delights in him!"

  9 Yet you drew me out of the womb,
    and made me safe on my mother's breast.
  10 I have been cast on your care since my birth;
    from my mother's womb you have been my God.
  11 Do not be far from me, for trouble is at hand;
    be near, for there is no one to help.

B 12 Many are the bulls that encircle me;
    fierce ones of Bashan surround me.
  13 Like ravenous and roaring lions,
    they open wide their jaws at me.

  14 My life is pouring out like water,
    and all my bones are out of joint;
    my heart within my breast melts like wax.
  15 My palate is dried up like a potsherd,
    and my tongue sticks to the roof of my mouth.
    You have laid me in the dust of death.

16   Packs of dogs close in on me;
    a gang of villains encircle me.
    They pierce my hands and my feet.
17   I can count all my bones,
    as they glare and gloat over me.
18   They divide my garments among them,
    and cast lots for my clothes.

19   Be not far off from me, LORD;
    You are my strength, hasten to help me.
20   [Save me from the sword,
    my life from the power of the dog.
21   Save me from the mouth of the lion,
    and from the horns of the wild oxen.]

    O God, answer me!

II

C 22   I shall proclaim your Name to my brothers;
    in the midst of the assembly I shall praise you.
25   My praise shall be of you in the great assembly;
    I will pay my vows among those who revere you:

23   Praise the LORD, you who fear him!
    Give him glory, you offspring of Jacob!
    Stand in awe of him, you children of Israel!

24   He does not despise the poor in his need,
    nor does he hide his face from him;
    but when he cries out, he hears him.

26   The poor will eat and be satisfied;
    those who seek the LORD will praise him.
    Long may they live!

D 27   Let all the ends of the earth remember
            and turn to the LORD.
        Let all the families of the nations
            do homage before him.

28   For the kingdom is the LORD's,
            and he rules over the nations.

29   Before him all who sleep in the earth bow down,
            and all who go down to the dust.

30   Our posterity will serve him,
            and tell of the LORD to coming generations.

31   They shall proclaim to a people yet unborn
            the deeds that he has done.

ANTIPHONS

Part I

Verse 1: Isa. 53:3
  He was despised and rejected,
    a man of sorrows and acquainted with grief.

Part II
Verse 25

A 1   The LORD is my shepherd;
         nothing can I want.

    2   He gives me rest in green pastures,
         leads me by quiet waters.

    3   He revives my spirit and guides me in right paths,
         for his Name's sake.

B 4   Though I walk through valleys of darkness,
         I fear no evil.
      You are always beside me with your club and staff
         to protect me.

    5   You spread out a banquet before me
         in sight of my foes.
      You anoint my head with perfume;
         my cup overflows.

    6   Surely your goodness and mercy follow me
         all my life long;
      And I will dwell in the house of the LORD,
         now and for ever.

ANTIPHONS

Verse 1: General.

John 10:11:
I am the good shepherd;
    the good shepherd lays down his life for the sheep.

Isa. 40:11:
He will feed his flock like a shepherd;
    he will gather the lambs in his arms.

I

1   The whole earth is the LORD's,
        the world and all who live in it.

2   He has founded it upon the seas,
        and set it firm above the deep waters.

3   "Who can ascend the LORD's mountain?
        Who can stand in his holy place?"

4   "Only one who has clean hands and a pure heart,
        who is not given to deceit nor sworn to lies.

5   He alone shall receive the LORD's blessing,
        and just reward from the God of his salvation."

6   Such are the people who seek him,
        who seek the God of Jacob face to face.

II

7   Lift up your heads, O gates!
    Open wide, you everlasting doors!
        Let the King of glory come in.

8   "Who is the King of glory?"
        "The LORD of power and might,
        The LORD, mighty in battle."

9   Lift up your heads, O gates!
    Open wide, you everlasting doors!
        Let the King of glory come in.

10   "Who is the King of glory?"
        "The LORD of power and might,
        He is the King of glory."

ANTIPHONS

Part I
Verse 1: General.
Verse 7: Advent.
Part II: Ascension.
John 12:32:
When I am lifted up from the
    earth,
  I will draw all men to myself.
John 13:31:
Now is the Son of Man glorified,
    and God is glorified in him.

Heb. 9:12a, 7:25b:
Christ has entered once for all
the holy place,
    and always lives to make
    intercession for us.
1 Peter 1:21:
God raised him from the dead
and gave him glory,
    so that your faith and hope
    are in God.

1   To you, Lord, I lift up my heart:

2   My God, I trust in you; let me not be put to shame;
        nor let my foes exult over me.
3   Let none who hope in you be put to shame;
        let them be shamed who are treacherous without cause.

4   Make me know your ways, Lord,
        and teach me your paths.
5   Lead me in your truth and teach me;
        for you are the God of my salvation,
        in whom I put my trust all the day long.

6   Remember, Lord, your mercy and love,
        for they have been ever from of old.
7   Remember not the sins of my youth or my offenses;
        according to your love remember me,
        for the sake of your goodness, Lord.

8   The Lord is good and upright;
        therefore he teaches sinners his way.
9   He guides the humble in what is right,
        and teaches the humble his way.

10   All the paths of the Lord are love and faithfulness,
        for those who keep his covenant and his precepts.
11   For the sake of your Name, Lord,
        forgive my sin, for it is great.

12   Who are they that fear the Lord?
        He will teach them the way they should choose.
13   They will dwell in prosperity,
        and their descendants will inherit the land.

14   The Lord is close to those who revere him,
        and makes known to them his covenant.
15   My eyes are ever looking toward the Lord;
        he will pull my feet clear of the net.

16   Turn to me and have pity on me,
        for I am alone and in misery.
17   The troubles of my heart are many;
        bring me out of my distress.

18   Look upon my affliction and misery,
     and forgive me all my sin.

19   Look at my enemies, how many they are,
     how violent their hatred is for me.

20   Protect my life and rescue me;
     let me not be shamed, for in you I have my hope.

21   Let my protection be integrity and uprightness;
     for in you I have placed my hope.

22   O God, redeem Israel,
     out of all their troubles.

ANTIPHONS

Verses 1–2: Advent.

Verses 6 and 22: Lent.

Other verses, as appropriate.

I

A   1   The Lord is my light and my salvation:
                          whom shall I fear?
        The Lord is the strength of my life:
                          of whom shall I be afraid?

     2   When evil-doers press hard upon me,
                          to devour me,
        It is they, my foes and adversaries,
                          who stumble and fall.

     3   Though an army encamp against me,
                          my heart will not fear;
        Though they raise up war against me,
                          yet my trust is in him.

B   4   One thing I ask of the Lord;
                          one thing I seek:
        That I may dwell in the house of the Lord
                          all the days of my life,
        To behold the beauty of the Lord,
                          to consult in his temple.

     5   For he will shelter me under his tent,
                          in the day of trouble.
        He will hide me secretly in his dwelling,
                          and set me high on a rock.

     6   Now is my head lifted up—
                          above my foes round about.
        Therefore I shall offer sacrifices in his tent
                        with shouts of joy;
        I will sing and make melody
                        to the Lord.

II

C   7   Hear my voice, Lord, when I cry;
                        have mercy and answer me.
     8   You have said to my heart, "Seek my face!"
                        your face, Lord, do I seek.
     9   Do not hide your face from me,
                        nor turn me away in anger.

[9a] You have been my help; do not cast me off or forsake me,
O God of my salvation!

10 Though my father and mother have forsaken me,
the LORD will uphold me.

D 11 Teach me your way, O LORD;
guide me on a level path
because of my enemies.

12 Deliver me not into the will of my foes;
false witnesses have risen against me,
such as those who breath violence.

13 I do believe that I shall see
the goodness of the LORD
in the land of the living.

14 Put your hope in the LORD.
Be strong and take courage.
Put your hope in the LORD.

ANTIPHONS

Verses 1 and 4: General.

Verse 5: Holy Week.

Verse 8: Lent.

Verse 13: Burial.

A 1   Give to the LORD glory, you heavens;
        give to the LORD glory and power.
   2   Give to the LORD glory due his Name;
        worship the LORD in his holy courts.

B *[2a]*   The God of glory thunders!
        The LORD hews flames of fire!

   3   The voice of the LORD is over the waters,
        the LORD over the sea waters.
   4   The voice of the LORD in might;
        the voice of the LORD in splendor.

  [4a]   The God of glory thunders!
        The LORD hews flames of fire!

   5   The voice of the LORD shatters the cedar trees;
        the LORD shatters the cedars of Lebanon.
   6   The voice of the LORD makes Lebanon skip like a calf,
        and Sirion like a young wild ox.

   7   The God of glory thunders!
        The LORD hews flames of fire!

   8   The voice of the LORD shakes the desert,
        the LORD shakes the desert of Kadesh.
   9   The voice of the LORD makes the oak trees writhe,
        and strips the forests bare.

  [9a]   Everyone in his temple shouts:
        Glory! Glory!

C 10   The LORD is enthroned above the waters;
        the LORD is enthroned King for evermore.
  11   The LORD gives strength to his people;
        the LORD blesses his people with peace.

ANTIPHONS

The refrain before verses 3, 5, and 8, or the praise
shout before verse 10.
Acts 2:1-3: When the day of Pentecost had come,
        they were all together in one place.
    From heaven came a sound of a rushing wind,
        and there appeared to them fiery tongues.

A   1   In you, O LORD, I take refuge;
     let me never be put to shame.

   [1a]   In your righteousness deliver me;
     bend your ear to me and hasten to save me.

   2   You are the rock of my refuge,
     a strong fortress where I am safe.

   3   You are my crag and my stronghold;
     for your Name's sake lead me and guide me.

   4   Get me out of the net they have hidden for me,
     for you are my tower of strength.

   5   Into your hand I commend my life, O LORD;
     you will redeem me, O God of truth.

   6   I hate those who put faith in empty idols;
     for I am one who trusts in the LORD.

   7   I rejoice and exult in your love,
     for you have seen my affliction and distress.

   8   You have not handed me over to my enemies,
     but have set my feet in a wide place.

B   9   Have mercy upon me, O LORD,
     for I am in trouble.

   [9a]   My eyes are become weak from grief,
     my soul and body are wasted.

   10   My life is worn out with sorrow,
     and my years with sighs.

   [10a]   My strength gives way in my suffering,
     and my bones decay.

   11   I have become a reproach to my foes,
     a fright to my friends.

   [11a]   Those who meet me in the street
     hurry on to pass me.

   12   I am forgotten, out of mind, like a corpse
     a broken and discarded jar.

   13   For I have heard the whispers of many;
     terror is all around me,

   [13a]   As they scheme together against me,
     plotting to take my life.

C   14   As for me, I have trusted in you, O LORD,
     and have said, "You are my God!"

15   My times are in your hand; deliver me
        from my foes and persecutors.
16   Let your face shine upon your servant,
        and save me in your loving-kindness.

17   LORD, let me not be ashamed, for I call upon you;
        instead, let the wicked be put to shame.
[17a] Let them be silenced in the grave,
        and their lying lips be made dumb;
18   For they speak insolently against the righteous,
        in their pride and their contempt.

19   How great is your goodness, O LORD,
        laid in store for those who fear you,
[19a] Which you do in the sight of all,
        for those who put their trust in you.
20   In the covert of your presence you hide them
        from the slanders of men.
[20a] You keep them safe in your shelter
        from the strife of tongues.

D 21   Blessed be the LORD,
            for his wonderful love
            to me in a besieged city.

   22   I said in my alarm,
            "You have cast me off from your sight";
            yet you heard the voice of my plea,
            when I called to you for help.

   23   Love the LORD, all you worshippers;
            the LORD protects his faithful ones.
            He will repay to the full
            those who are arrogant.

   24   Be strong; let your hearts have courage,
            all you who hope in the LORD.

ANTIPHONS
Verses 1, 5, 9, or 15: Holy Week, General.

1   Shout for joy to the LORD, you righteous;
       praise is becoming to the upright.

2   Praise the LORD with the harp;
       make music to him on the ten-stringed lyre.

3   Sing to him a song that is new;
       play with skill and with a loud shout.

4   For the word of the LORD is just;
       all his deeds are worthy of trust.

5   He loves righteousness and justice;
       the LORD fills the earth with his goodness.

6   By the word of the LORD were the heavens made;
       and all their hosts by the breath of his mouth.

7   He gathers the great waters in a bottle,
       the deeps of the sea in his storeroom.

8   Let all the earth fear the LORD,
       all the dwellers in the world stand in awe of him.

9   He speaks and it comes into being;
       he commands and it is established.

10   The LORD overturns the counsel of the nations,
       and brings to nought the plans of the peoples.

11   For the LORD's will stands fast for ever;
       and the designs of his heart from age to age.

12   Blest is the nation whose God is the LORD,
       and the people he has chosen for his heritage.

13   The LORD looks down from heaven,
       and sees all the human race.

14   From where he is enthroned he looks out
       upon all who inhabit the earth.

15   He molded the hearts of all of them,
       and discerns all their doings.

16   No king is saved by a great army,
       nor a warrior by mighty strength.

17   A horse is a vain hope for victory;
       for all its strength, it cannot save.

18   For the eye of the LORD is on those who fear him,
       on those who hope in his love,

19   That he may save them from death,
       and keep them alive in famine.

20   The hope of our life is in the LORD;
       he is our help and our shield.

21   For in him our heart rejoices;
       in his holy Name we put our trust.

22   Let your loving-kindness, O LORD, be over us,
       even as we have put our hope in you.

ANTIPHONS

Verses 1 or 22: General.

Verses 18-19*a* or 20-21: Easter.

Psalm 34

A 1   I will bless the LORD at all times;
           his praise shall be ever in my mouth.
   2   In the LORD I will make my boast;
           let the humble hear and rejoice.

   3   Magnify the LORD with me;
           let us together exalt his Name.
   4   I sought the LORD and he answered me,
           and delivered me from all my fears.

   5   Look to him, and you will be radiant;
           and your faces will not be ashamed.
   6   This poor one called and the LORD heard,
           and I was saved from all my troubles.

   7   The LORD's angel encamps about those who fear him,
           and he will deliver them.
   8   Taste and see that the LORD is good;
           happy are they who trust in him.

   9   Fear the LORD, you saints of his;
           for those who fear him want nothing.
  10   The lions suffer want and hunger;
           those who seek the LORD want nothing that is good.

B 11   Come, children, and listen to me;
           and I will teach you to fear the LORD.
  12   Who is there that loves life;
           who desires a long life to enjoy prosperity?

  13   Keep your tongue from speaking evil,
           and your lips from telling lies.
  14   Turn from evil and do what is good;
           seek peace and pursue it.

  15   The LORD's eyes are open to the righteous,
           and his ears open to their prayer.
  16   The LORD's face is against evil-doers,
           to cut off their remembrance from the earth.

  17   When the righteous call, the LORD hears them,
           and rescues them from all their troubles.
  18   The LORD is near the broken in heart,
           and saves those who are crushed in spirit.

19 The righteous have many troubles,
    but the LORD rescues them out of all.
20 He will keep all of their bones safe;
    not one of them will be broken.

21 Evil will bring death to the wicked;
    those who hate the righteous will be punished.
22 The LORD will redeem the life of his servants;
    none who trust in him will be condemned.

ANTIPHONS
Verses 1, 11, 15, or 22, or any other verse as appropriate.

(Verses 5-10)

5   Your loving-kindness, O LORD, reaches to the heavens,
      and your faithfulness to the clouds.

6   Your righteousness is strong as the mountains,
      and your judgments vast as the deeps.
      You, LORD, save man and beast.

7   How priceless is your love, O God;
      we take refuge under the shadow of your wings;

8   We feast on the rich abundance of your house,
      and drink from the river of your pleasures.

9   For with you is the fountain of life;
      and in your light we see light.

10   Continue your goodness to those who know you,
      and your justice to those true of heart.

ANTIPHONS

Verse 7: General.

John 1:4-5:
In him was life,
    and the life was the light of men.
The light shines in the darkness,
    and the darkness has not overcome it.

A   1   As a deer pants for the water-brooks,
   so longs my soul for you, O God.

 2   My soul thirsts for God, for the living God;
   how long before I come and behold his face?

 3   My tears have been my food day and night,
   while they say to me all day long,
   "Where now is your God?"

 4   As I pour out my soul, I remember
   how I went with the throngs,
   and led them into the house of God,

[4a]   With shouts of praise and thanksgiving,
   among the crowds keeping festival.

 5   Why are you down cast, my soul?
   why so distraught within me?
  Put your trust in God;
   I shall again praise him,
   my help and my God.

B   6   My soul is down cast within me;
   for I remember you from the land of Jordan,
   the little hill from the heights of Hermon.

 7   Deeps call up deeps at the roar of your waterfalls;
   all your billows and torrents go over me.

 8   By day and by night his song is with me,
   a prayer to the God of my life.

 9   I will say to God, my rock:
   "Why have you forgotten me?
   Why do I mourn because my foes oppress me?"

 10 My bones break as my enemies mock me,
   while they say to me all day long,
   "Where now is your God?"

 11 Why are you down cast, my soul?
   why so distraught within me?
  Put your trust in God;
   I shall again praise him,
   my help and my God.

C 1   Give judgment for me, O God;
         plead my cause against a godless people,
         and rescue me from the deceitful and wicked.

    2   O God, you are my stronghold; why cast me off?
         why let me mourn while my foes oppress me?

    3   Send out your light and your truth to lead me,
         and bring me to your holy hill and dwelling;

    4   That I may go to the altar of God,
         to the God of my joy and gladness.

 [4a]   On the harp I will give you thanks,
         O God, my God.

    5   Why are you down cast, my soul?
            why so distraught within me?
          Put your trust in God;
            I shall again praise him,
            my help and my God.

ANTIPHONS

Verse 1: Baptism.

Verses 3-4, Strophe C: Eucharist.

Verses 5, 11, and 5 (Strophe C): General.

1   God is our refuge and strength,
      an ever ready help in time of trouble.
2   We shall not fear if the earth is shaken,
      if the mountains fall into the deeps of the sea;
3   Even if the waters rage and foam,
      and the mountains quake in the surging tide.

[3a]   The mighty LORD is with us;
      the God of Jacob is our fortress.

4   There are river-streams that make glad the city of God,
      the holy dwelling place of the Most High.
5   God is in her midst; she cannot be shaken.
      God will help her at the breaking of dawn.
6   Nations are in tumult and kingdoms are tottering;
      God speaks and the earth melts away.

7   The mighty LORD is with us;
      the God of Jacob is our fortress.

8   Come, see the works of the LORD,
      the awesome deeds he has done in the earth.
9   He puts an end to wars in all the world;
      he breaks the bow and shatters the spear,
      and burns up the chariots with fire.
10   "Be still and know that I am God;
      I am exalted among the nations,
      I am exalted in the earth."

11   The mighty LORD is with us;
      the God of Jacob is our fortress.

ANTIPHONS

Verses *[3a]*, 7 and 11: General.

Rev. 21:1-2:

I saw a new heaven and a new earth,
  and I saw the holy city, the new Jerusalem,
  coming down out of heaven from God.

Psalm 47

A   1   Clap your hands, clap your hands, all you peoples;
           shout to God, shout to God with songs of joy!

       2   The LORD, the Most High, is awesome;
           he is a great King over all the world.

       3   He subdues the peoples under us,
           and makes the nations subject to us.

       4   He has chosen for us our inheritance,
           the glory of Jacob whom he loves.

       5   God has gone up with a shout,
           the LORD with a blast of the horn.

B   6   Sing praises, sing praises to God;
           sing praises, sing praises to our King!

       7   For God is King over all the world;
           sing praises to him with psalms.

       8   God reigns over the nations;
           God is seated on his holy throne.

       9   The rulers of the peoples are assembled
           with the people of the God of Abraham.

     10   Their ensigns belong to our God,
           who is great and exalted above all.

ANTIPHONS

Verse 5: Ascension.

Eph. 4:8:

When he ascended on high,
   he led captivity captive,
   and gave gifts to men.

A   1   Great is the LORD,
        and great be his praise,
  [1a] in the city of our God,
        his holy mountain.
    2   Fairest among hills,
        joy of the whole earth,
  [2a] Mount Zion, summit of the world,
        and city of the great King!
    3   God is in her palaces,
        and known as her fortress.

B   4   Lo, kings assembled together,
        in rage marched against her.
    5   They saw her and were astounded;
        terror-stricken they fled.
    6   Trembling seized them there,
        anguish as one in travail;
    7   shattered like the ships of Tarshish,
        blown by the east wind.
    8   What we have heard, now we have seen
        in the city of the LORD of hosts,
  [8a] in the city of our God,
        established by God for ever.

C   9   O God, we have pondered your love
        in the midst of your temple.
   10   Your praise, O God, like your Name
        reaches the ends of the world.
 [10a] Your right hand is full of justice—
        let Mount Zion rejoice,
   11   and the cities of Judah exult,
        because of your judgments.

   12   Walk about Zion, all around her,
        and count her towers.
   13   Consider her ramparts,
        examine her palaces.

14   So you may tell the next generation
                that this is our God,
[14a]   our God for ever and ever;
                he will be our guide.

ANTIPHONS

Verses 10 or 14: Pentecost.

Ps. 87:3:

Glorious things are spoken of you,
    O city of our God.

Rev. 21:2-3:

I saw the holy city, new Jerusalem,
    coming down out of heaven from God.

And I heard a great voice saying,
    "Behold, the dwelling of God is with men,
    He will dwell with them, and they shall
        be his people."

A 1   The Lord, the God of gods, has spoken;
        he has summoned the earth
        from the rising of the sun to its setting.

    2   Out of Zion, perfect in beauty,
        God shines with glory.

    3   Our God will come and will not be silent;
        before him there is a consuming fire,
        and round about him is a raging storm.

    4   He calls heaven and earth from above,
        to witness the judgment of his people:

    5   "Assemble before me my servants,
        who made a covenant with me by sacrifice."

    6   Let the heavens proclaim his justice,
        for God himself is the Judge.

B 7   "Hear, my people, and I shall speak;
        Israel, I shall witness against you.
[7a]   For I am God, your God,
        [who brought you up out of Egypt.]"

    8   "I do not accuse you because of your sacrifices;
        your offerings are always before me.

    9   I shall take no bull-calf from your herds,
        nor any rams from your corrals.

   10   For every creature of the forest is mine,
        and the cattle in their thousands upon the hills.

   11   I know all the birds of the sky;
        whatever moves in the fields is mine.

   12   If I were hungry, I would not tell you,
        since everything in the world belongs to me.

   13   Do you think I eat the flesh of bulls,
        or drink the blood of rams?

   14   Let thanksgiving be your sacrifice to God,
        and make good your vows to the Most High.

   15   Call on me in the day of trouble,
        I will deliver you, and you will honor me."

Psalm 50

C 16   To the wicked, God says:

"What right have you to recite my commandments,
    and take my covenant on your lips?
17   For you despise my discipline,
    and toss my words behind you.

18   When you see a thief, you make a friend of him,
    and throw in your lot with adulterers.
19   Your conversation is full of evil,
    and your tongue in inventing lies.

20   You sit there maligning your brother,
    and slandering your mother's son.
21   You have done these things; shall I be silent
    because you think that I am like yourself?

D [21a]   I have made my case against you,
    and have set it before your eyes.
22   Mark it well, you who forget God,
    lest I rend you and none deliver you.
23   Whoever offers me the sacrifice of thanksgiving
    does me honor;
    And to him who heeds my way I shall show
    the salvation of God."

ANTIPHONS
Verse 2: Advent.
Verse 23: General.

1   Have mercy on me, O God, in your loving-kindness;
       in your compassion blot out my offenses.
2   Wash me thoroughly from my iniquity,
       and cleanse me from my sin.

3   I know full well my misdeeds,
       and my sin is ever before me.
4   Against you, against you only, have I sinned,
       and done what is evil in your sight.

[4a]   You are just in your sentence,
       and righteous in your judgment.
5   I was conceived in iniquity,
       and a sinner from my mother's womb.

6   Yet you look for truth in my inmost being,
       and teach me wisdom in my heart.
7   Purify me that I may be clean;
       wash me, make me whiter than snow.

8   Let me hear joy and gladness,
       that the bones you have broken may rejoice.
9   Hide not your face from my sins,
       and wipe out all my iniquity.

10   Create in me a pure heart, O God,
       and renew a right spirit within me.
11   Cast me not away from your presence,
       and take not your holy Spirit from me.

12   Restore to me the joy of your salvation,
       and uphold me in a free will of obedience,
13   That I may teach transgressors your ways,
       and turn sinners back to you.

14   Deliver me from death, O God my savior,
       that my tongue may sing of your justice.
15   O Lord, open my lips,
       and my mouth shall proclaim your praise.

16   You have no delight in sacrifices;
       a burnt-offering from me would not please you.
17   The sacrifice you accept is a humble spirit;
       a broken and contrite heart, O God, you will not reject.

18   In your goodness show favor to Zion;
        rebuild the walls of Jerusalem.
19   Then you will be pleased with right offerings
        and the young bulls brought to your altar.

ANTIPHONS

Verses 7, 10, or 17.

Isa. 55:6-7:

Seek the LORD while he may be found;
    call upon him while he is near.
Return to the LORD, that he may have mercy,
    and to our God, for he will abundantly pardon.

A   1   Be merciful to me, O God, be merciful,
          for in you my spirit takes refuge.
  [1a] I will take refuge in the shadow of your wings,
          until this ravaging has passed.
    2   I will call upon God Most High,
          to God who does what is good for me.
    3   He will send from heaven and save me,
          and put to shame those who trample upon me.
  [3a]   God will send forth his love
          and his faithfulness.

B   4   I lie in the midst of lions,
          greedy for human prey;
  [4a]   their teeth are spears and arrows,
          and their tongues are sharp swords.
    6   They have laid a net for my feet,
          in order to lay me low;
  [6a]   they have dug a pit before me,
          but have fallen into it themselves.

C   5   Exalt yourself, O God, above the heavens;
          let your glory be over all the earth.

    7   O God, my heart is ready,
          my heart is ready.
          I will sing and make melody.

    8   Awake, my spirit;
          awake, lute and harp.
          I will awake the dawn.

    9   I will praise you, O Lord, among the peoples;
          I will make melody to you among the nations.
   10   For your love is higher than the heavens,
          and your faithfulness reaches to the skies.

   11   Exalt yourself, O God, above the heavens;
          let your glory be over all the earth.

ANTIPHONS

Verse 3: Holy Week, strophes A and B.

Verses 5 and 11: Holy Week, strophe C, and General.

Psalm 65

A 1   You are worthy to be praised, O God, in Zion;
        to you shall vows be performed in Jerusalem.

    2   O Hearer of prayer, to you shall all flesh come,
        because of their transgressions.

    3   Our sins are too heavy for us;
        but you will blot them out.

    4   Blest are they whom you choose and draw near
        to dwell in your courts.

[4a]   They will be satisfied with the goodness
        of your house, your holy temple.

    5   You show us the wonders of your righteousness,
        O God of our salvation.

[5a]   You are the hope of the most distant lands,
        and of the isles in the farthest seas.

    6   By your strength you made fast the mountains,
        and girded them about with might.

    7   You still the raging of the sea-waves,
        and the tumults of the peoples.

    8   Those who dwell in the farthermost regions
        stand in awe of your marvels.

[8a]   When you make the dawn and the dusk,
        they shout for joy.

B 9   You visit the earth with abundant water,
        and make it burst forth with plenty.

[9a]   The river of God is full of water,
        to prepare and provide for the grain.

    10   You drench the furrows and level the ridges,
        with showers to soften the earth
        and bless the increase of it.

    11   You crown the year with your bounty;
        your pathways pour with plenteousness.

    12   The fields are wet in the wilderness,
        and the hills are girded with joy.

    13   The pastures are covered with flocks;
        the valleys are decked with wheat;
        they shout, they sing for joy.

ANTIPHONS

Verse 1: General.

Verse 9: Rogation Days.

Verse 11: Thanksgiving Day.

Ps. 67:6:
The earth has yielded its increase;
    God, our own God, has blessed us.

I

A 1   Raise a shout to God, all the earth;
    2   sing the glory of his Name,
           make his praise glorious.
    3   Say to God: "How awesome are your deeds!
           So great is your power;
           your enemies cringe before you.
    4   All the earth worships you;
           to you they sing praises,
           they sing praises to your Name."

B 5   Come, see the works of God,
           his awesome deeds among us.
    6   He turned the sea into dry land,
           so they went through the water on foot.
    7   There we rejoiced in him,
           who rules by his might for ever.
[7a] His eyes keep watch over the nations;
           let no rebels rise up against him.

C 8   Bless our God, you peoples,
           make the sound of his praise to be heard;
    9   For he keeps us among the living,
           and does not allow our feet to stumble.
  10   Yet you have tested us, O God,
           tried us the way silver is refined.
  11   You brought us into a trap-net;
           you laid grievous burdens on our backs.
  12   You have allowed men to ride over us prostrate;
           we have gone through fire and water.
           Yet you brought us out into a place of liberty.

D 13   I will enter your house with burnt-offerings,
           and I will pay you my vows,
  14   Which my lips promised and my mouth spoke,
           when I was in trouble.
  15   I will give you fatlings in sacrifice,
           together with the smoke of rams,
           and offerings of oxen and goats.

E 16   Come and hear, all you who fear God;
           I will tell you what he has done for me.

17   I cried out to him with my mouth,
           and extolled him with my tongue.

18   Had I cherished any evil in my heart,
           the LORD would not have heard me.

19   Yet in truth God did hear me,
           and gave heed to the voice of my prayer.

20   Blessed be God, who has not rejected my prayer,
           nor turned away his love from me.

ANTIPHONS

Verse 12c: Easter, General.

Easter:
Alleluia! The Lord is risen.
    The Lord is risen indeed. Alleluia!

A 1   God be gracious to us and bless us;
               may the light of your face shine upon us,

     2   That your ways may be known on the earth,
               your salvation among all nations.

     3   Let the peoples praise you, O God.
               Let all the peoples praise you.

B 4   Let the nations exult in you,
               and shout with joy;
  [4a] For with justice you judge the peoples,
               and rule the nations of the earth.

     5   Let the peoples praise you, O God.
               Let all the peoples praise you.

C 6   The earth has yielded its increase;
               God, our own God, has blessed us.
     7   May God continue to give us his blessing,
               until all the ends of the earth worship him.

  [7a]   Let the peoples praise you, O God.
               Let all the peoples praise you.

ANTIPHONS

The refrain of verses 3, 5, and [7a].

A   1   Save me, O God!
          the waters threaten my life.

    2   I sink down in the mire,
          and there is no foothold.
  [2a] I have come into deep waters;
          the flood closes over me.

    3   I am worn out with my crying;
          my throat is parched.
  [3a] My eyes are failing me,
          waiting for my God.

    4   More than the hairs of my head are they
          who hate me without cause.
  [4a] Powerful are they who would destroy me,
          and who attack me with lies.

  [4b] Why should I now restore
          what I never stole?
    5   O God, you know my foolishness;
          my sins are not hid from you.

B   6   LORD God of might, let not those who hope in you
          be ashamed because of me.
  [6a] O God of Israel, let not those who seek you
          be disgraced because of me.

    7   For your sake I have suffered reproach,
          and shame has covered my face.
    8   I have become a stranger to my brothers,
          an alien to my mother's sons.

    9   Zeal for your house has consumed me;
          the taunts against you fall on me.
   10   I humbled myself with fasting,
          but it turned to my reproach.

   11   I clothed myself in sackcloth,
          and became a byword among them.
   12   They who sit at the gate talk of me;
          drunkards make songs about me.

C 13   My prayer to you, LORD, is at a time
                that is pleasing to you.
[13a]   In your great mercy, O God, answer me
                with your steadfast love.

14   Save me from sinking in the mire;
                deliver me from my enemies.
[14a]   Rescue me from the deep waters,
                lest the flood swallow me.

15   Let not the deep torrents overwhelm me,
                or the grave close its mouth on me.
16   Answer me, LORD, for your loving-kindness;
                turn to me in your mercy.

17   Hide not your face from your servant;
                in my distress answer me swiftly.
18   Draw near to me and save me;
                free me from my enemies.

19   You know how they abuse and dishonor me;
                all my foes are known to you.
20   Their reproach has broken my heart;
                I am grievously ill.

[20a]   I looked for sympathy and for comforters;
                but I could find none.
21   They put bitter poison in my food,
                and gave me vinegar for my thirst.

29   Yet though I am afflicted and in pain,
                your help, O God, lifts me high.

D 30   I will praise the Name of God in song,
                and extol him with thanksgiving.
31   This pleases the LORD more than an ox,
                or a bullock with horns and hoofs.

32   The humble will see it and be glad;
                you that seek God, revive your heart.
33   For the LORD listens to the needy;
                his prisoners he does not despise.

34   The heavens and the earth will praise him,
         the sea and all that moves in it.
35   For God will save Zion,
         and rebuild the cities of Judah.

[35a] His servants will live there and possess it;
         their offspring will inherit it.
36   All those who love his Name
         will dwell therein.

ANTIPHONS

The first verse of each strophe, or others as appropriate to the psalm
  as a whole.

See also the antiphons for Psalm 22.

Psalm 72

A 1   Give your justice to the King, O God,
        and your righteousness to the King's Son;
    2   That he may judge your people with right,
        and the poor and afflicted with justice.

    3   By his righteousness may the people have peace,
        upon the mountains and the little hills.
    4   May he defend the poor among the people,
        save the needy and crush the oppressor.

    5   May his life continue as long as the sun,
        and as the moon, through all generations.
    6   May he descend like the rain on the mown fields,
        and like showers that water the earth.

    7   In his days may righteousness flourish,
        and peace abound till the moon be no more.
    8   May his rule be from sea to sea,
        from the River to the ends of the earth.

    9   May his foes bow down before him,
        and his enemies lick the dust.
   10   May the kings of Tarshish and the isles pay tribute,
        and the kings of Arabia and Saba offer gifts.

   11   May all kings do obeisance before him,
        and all nations give him service.
   12   For he will deliver the poor who cry out to him,
        the afflicted and oppressed who have no helper.

   13   He will take pity upon the weak and the poor,
        and will save the lives of the needy.
   14   He will rescue them from oppression and violence,
        for their blood is precious in his sight.

B 15   Long may he live!
        and may the gold of Arabia be given him.
        May prayer be made for him without ceasing;
        may they bless him all the day long.

   16   May there be an abundance of grain in the land,
        even to the hill-tops;
        And may fruit be luxuriant as Lebanon,
        and flourish as the grass of the field.

17   May his name be established for ever,
    as long as the sun endures.
  In him may all peoples be blest,
    and all nations called him blessed.

18   [Blessed be the LORD, the God of Israel,
    who alone does wondrous deeds.
19   Blessed be his glorious Name for ever;
    let his glory fill the whole earth!
    Amen! Amen!]

ANTIPHONS

Verses 11-12: Epiphany.

Doxology of verses 18-19: General.

A 1   O Shepherd of Israel, give ear,
      you that leads Joseph like a flock;
      shine forth from your throne on the cherubim.

   2   Before Ephraim, Benjamin and Manasseh
      Stir up your power!
      Come to save us!

   3   Lord God of might, restore us;
      let your face shine and we shall be saved.

B   4   O Lord God of might, how long will you be angry
      with the prayers of your people?

   5   You have fed them with tears for bread,
      and given them abundant tears to drink.

   6   You have made us a mockery to our neighbors,
      and our enemies laugh us to scorn.

   7   Lord God of might, restore us;
      let your face shine and we shall be saved.

C   8   You brought out a vine from Egypt;
      you drove out the nations and planted it.

   9   You cleared the ground for it;
      it took root and filled the land.

  10   The mountains were covered by its shade,
      and the mighty cedars with its branches.

  11   It stretched out its tendrils to the Sea,
      and its shoots to the River.

  12   Why have you broken down its wall,
      so that all who pass by may pluck it?

  13   The wild boar of the forest ravages it;
      the wild creatures of the field feed on it.

[14]   Lord God of might, restore us;
      let your face shine and we shall be saved.

D 15   Look down from heaven and see this vine;
      attend to what your right hand has planted.

  16   They have burned it and cut it down;
      may they perish at the rebuke of your face!

17   Let your hand be on the One you favor,
       the Son you have made strong for yourself.

18   So we will not turn back from you again;
       revive us that we may call on your Name.

19   LORD God of might, restore us;
       let your face shine and we shall be saved.

ANTIPHONS

Verses 3, 7, *[14]*, and 19: Advent.

A 1 How lovely is your dwelling place,
         O Lord of might!

    2 My soul longs and faints
         for the courts of the Lord.
      My whole being rejoices
         in the living God.

    3 The sparrow finds a home,
         the swallow a nest,
      Where she may lay her young,
         near your altars,
      O Lord of might,
         my King and my God.

B 4 Blest are they who dwell in your house,
         ever singing your praise!

    5 Blest are they who have in you their strength;
         in whose hearts are the highways to Zion!

    6 They go through a barren valley,
         and find it with springs;
      For the early rains
         have filled it with pools.
    7 They go from height to height;
         for the God of gods
         will be seen in Zion.

C 8 Lord God of might, hear my prayer;
         give ear to me, God of Jacob.

    9 Look with favor on our King, O God;
         behold the face of your Anointed.

   10 One day in your courts is better
         than a thousand elsewhere.
      I would rather stand at the door of God's house,
         than dwell in the tents of the wicked.

   11 For the Lord God is a sun and shield;
         the Lord bestows grace and glory.
      No good thing does the Lord withhold
         from those who live uprightly.

12   O Lᴏʀᴅ of might,
Blest is everyone
who trusts in you!

ANTIPHONS

Each strophe has its own antiphons at beginning
   and end; they may be used singly or in combination.

Ps. 26:8:

Lᴏʀᴅ, I love the house where you dwell,
   and the place where your glory abides.

Psalm 85

A 1   Lord, you once favored your land,
     and revived the fortunes of Jacob.

2   You pardoned the guilt of your people,
     and covered all their sins.

3   You retracted all your rage,
     and turned away from the heat of your anger.

4   Restore us now, God our Savior,
     and remove your grievance against us.

5   Will you be angry with us for ever,
     and prolong your wrath from age to age?

6   Will you not revive our life again,
     that your people may rejoice in you?

7   Lord, show us your love and mercy,
     and give us your saving help.

B 8   I am listening to what the Lord God is saying:

     He is speaking peace to his faithful people,
     and to those who turn their hearts to him.

9   His saving help is near those who fear him,
     that his glory may dwell in our land.

10   Mercy and truth have met together;
     righteousness and peace have kissed each other.

11   Truth shall sprout forth from the earth,
     and righteousness look down from heaven.

12   The Lord will give us prosperity;
     our land shall yield its harvests.

13   Righteousness shall march before him,
     and peace shall be the pathway of his feet.

ANTIPHONS
Verse 7: Advent; also sung after verse 13, if desired.

Preface

[The psalmist]

1   Your love, O LORD, will I sing for ever;
      I will proclaim your faithfulness to all generations.
2   I will say: "Your love will endure for ever;
      your faithfulness is set firmly in the heavens."

[The LORD]

3   I have made a covenant with my chosen One;
      I have sworn an oath to David my servant:
4   "I will confirm your dynasty for ever,
      and establish your throne for all generations."

I

A 5   Let the heavens praise your wonders, O LORD,
      and your faithfulness in the council of the gods.
6   Who in the skies can be compared to the LORD?
      who is like the LORD among the gods?

7   God is to be feared in the council of the gods,
      great and terrible to all those around him.
8   Who is like you, LORD, God of might?
      your power and faithfulness, O LORD, surround you.

9   You rule over the raging of the sea;
      when its waves ride high, you subdue them.
10 You crushed to death Rahab, the monster of the deep;
      with your mighty arm you scattered your foes.

11 The heavens are yours, and the earth also;
      the world and all that is in it you have founded.
12 You created the limits of the north and the south;
      Mounts Tabor and Hermon rejoice in your Name.

13 Your arm is mighty, your hand is strong;
      your right hand is lifted high.
14 Righteousness and justice are the foundation of your
        throne;
      love and faithfulness go ever before you.

B 15   Blest are the people who know the festal shout;
        they walk, O Lᴏʀᴅ, in the light of your presence.
  16   They rejoice all day long in your Name,
        and exult in your righteousness.

  17   You are the glory of our strength,
        and by your favor our honor is exalted;
  18   For our Shield belongs to the Lᴏʀᴅ,
        our King to the Holy One of Israel.

II

C 19   Once you spoke in a vision,
        and said to a faithful one:
[19a]   "I have set a crown upon a mighty warrior;
        I have exalted one chosen from the people.

  20   I have found David my servant;
        with my holy oil I have anointed him.
  21   My hand will hold him steady;
        my arm will give him strength.

  22   No enemy will be able to outwit him,
        nor any wicked one do him harm;
  23   For I will crush his foes before him,
        and strike down those who hate him.

  24   My faithfulness and love will be with him;
        through my Name his honor will be exalted.
  25   The dominion of his hands will extend
        from the Sea to the River.

  26   He will call to me: 'You are my Father,
        my God, and the rock of my salvation.'
  27   I shall make him my first-born,
        the highest of the kings of the earth.

  28   I will always keep my love for him,
        and my covenant with him will stand firm.
  29   I will establish his dynasty for ever;
        his throne will be as the days of heaven.

D 30   If his sons shall forsake my law,
        and do not live by my statutes;

31   If they violate my decrees,
        and do not observe my commandments,

32   I will punish their sins with a rod,
        and their offenses with a lash.

33   But I will never withdraw my love from him,
        or be false to my faithfulness.

34   I will not violate my covenant,
        nor alter the word that I spoke.

35   Once for all I have sworn by my holiness;
        I would not lie to David:

36   'Your dynasty shall endure for ever,
        and its throne like the sun before me.

37   Like the moon it is established for ever,
        and will stand firm as long as the skies.'"

III

E 38   Now you have cast off and rejected
        and are full of wrath against your Anointed.

39   You have broken the covenant with your servant;
        you have defiled his crown in the dust.

40   You have breached all his walls of defense,
        and laid all his strongholds in ruin.

41   All who pass by can plunder him;
        his neighbors treat him with contempt.

42   You have given his foes the advantage,
        and made all his enemies rejoice.

43   You have turned the edge of his sword,
        and failed to support him in battle.

44   You have put an end to his splendor,
        and his throne you have cast to the ground.

45   You have cut his days off in his prime,
        and covered him over with shame.

IV

F 46   How long, O Lord? Will you hide yourself for ever?
        How long will your wrath burn like fire?

47 Remember, O LORD, how short is our life,
    with what frailty you have created us.
48 Who can live and never see death,
    or save himself from the power of the grave?

49 Where, LORD, is your love from of old,
    the faithfulness you swore to David?
50 Remember, LORD, the disgrace of your servant,
    how I bear in my heart the taunts of the peoples,
51 How your foes insult you, O LORD,
    and mocked the retreat of your Anointed.

52   [Blessed be the LORD for ever!
    Amen and Amen!]

ANTIPHONS
Verses 1-2: Parts I and IV.
Verses 3-4: Parts II and III.
Verses 26-27: Christmas.

I

1   LORD, you have been our home and refuge
       from generation to generation.

2   Before the mountains were brought forth,
       or the earth and the world were formed,
       from ages to ages you are God.

3   Do not turn us back to the dust,
       or say, "Return, O children of men."

4   A thousand years in your sight
       are but a yesterday that is gone.

5   As a watch in the night or a fleeting dream,
       they are like grass that flourishes and fades.

6   In the morning it sprouts up and is green;
       in the evening it dries up and withers.

7   Are we to be consumed by your anger,
       or perish from your displeasure?

8   You have laid bare our iniquities before you,
       our secret sins in the light of your face.

9   All our days pass away in your anger;
       our years come to an end like a sigh.

10   The number of our years is but seventy,
       or even eighty if we are strong.

[10a]   Yet their span is but toil and trouble;
       they go swiftly and fly away.

11   Who understands the power of your anger;
       who fears aright your indignation?

12   So teach us to take account of our days,
       that we may give our hearts to wisdom.

II

13   How long, O LORD, before you return,
       and have pity on your servants?

14   Fill a new dawn with your loving-kindness,
        that we may shout for joy and gladness all our days.

15   Repay us for the days of our suffering,
        and the years when we were afflicted.

16   Show your wonders to your servants,
        and your glorious splendor to their children.

17   May the favor of the Lord our God be upon us;
        prosper, prosper the work of our hands!

ANTIPHONS

Verses 1-2 or 12: New Year's, Burial, General.

2 Peter 3:13:

According to his promise we look for a new heaven
and a new earth in which righteousness dwells.

Psalm 91

A 1   Whoever dwells under the shelter of the Most High,
           and abides in the shade of the Almighty,

    2   Shall say of the LORD, "My refuge, my fortress,
           my God in whom is my trust."

    3   For he rescues you from the hunter's snare,
           and from deadly pestilence.

    4   He covers you with his pinions,
           and under his wings you find refuge;
           his faithfulness is a shield and buckler.

B 5   You will not be afraid of terror in the night,
           nor of arrows that fly in the day—

    6   Neither the pestilence that stalks in the darkness,
           nor a sudden sickness that strikes at noon-time.

    7   A thousand may fall at your side,
           ten thousand at your right hand;
           but you will be unharmed.

    8   Your eyes have only to look
           and see the reward of the wicked.

C 9   Because you have made the LORD your refuge,
           and made the Most High your home,

   10   No evil will happen to you,
           nor calamity come near your dwelling.

   11   He will give charge over you to his angels,
           to guard you in all your ways.

   12   In their hands they will hold you,
           lest you stub your foot on a stone.

   13   You will tread on poisonous serpents;
           you will trample young lions and dragons.

D 14   Because he holds fast to me in love,
           I will save him;
         Because he knows my Name,
           I will protect him.

15   When he calls upon me,
        I will answer him.
    In trouble I will be with him;
        I will rescue and honor him.

16   With long life I will satisfy him,
        and show him my salvation.

ANTIPHONS

Verses 1-2 or 7: General.

Verses 11-12: Lent.

A   1   Come, let us sing to the Lord;
          let us shout for joy to the Rock of our salvation.

       2   Let us come before his presence with thanksgiving,
          and raise a loud shout to him in psalms.

       3   For the Lord is a great God,
          and a great King above all gods.

B   4   In his hand are the deep places of the earth,
          and the high peaks of the mountains are his also.

       5   The sea is his, for he made it;
          and his hands formed the dry land.

       6   Come, let us bow down and give homage,
          and kneel before the Lord our Maker.

       7   For he is our God;
          and we are his people,
          the sheep of his pasture.

Today will you listen to his voice?

C   8   "Harden not your hearts, as at Meribah,
          as on the day at Massah in the desert,

       9   When your fathers tried me and put me to the test,
          though they had seen the wonders I performed.

     10   Forty years long I loathed that generation,
          and said, 'The people are fickle in their hearts;
          they do not discern my ways.'

     11   So I swore in my anger,
          'They shall not enter the place of my rest.' "

ANTIPHONS

Verses 3 or 6: General.

Ps. 96:9:

Worship the Lord in the beauty of holiness;
   let the whole earth be in awe of him.

Psalm 96

A 1   Sing to the Lord a new song;
        sing to the Lord, all the earth,
    2   Sing to the Lord, bless his Name;
        proclaim his salvation from day to day.
    3   Tell out his glory among the nations,
        and his marvelous works to all peoples.

B 4   The Lord is great and worthy to be praised;
        he is awesome above all gods.
    5   The gods of the peoples are nothing but idols;
        but the Lord made the heavens.
    6   Glory and majesty surround him;
        power and splendor adorn his sanctuary.

C 7   Give to the Lord, you families of peoples;
        give to the Lord glory and power.
    8   Give to the Lord the honor due his Name;
        bring offerings and come into his courts.
    9   Worship the Lord in the beauty of holiness;
        let the whole earth dance before him.

D 10   Declare among the nations: "The Lord is King!
        he has established the world firm and immovable."
  11   Let the heavens rejoice and the earth be glad;
        let the sea resound, and everything in it.
  12   Let the fields be joyful and everything in them,
        and the trees of the wood shout for joy.

E 13   Before the Lord when he comes,
        when he comes to judge the earth.
       He will judge the world with justice,
        and the peoples with his truth.

ANTIPHONS

Verses 1 or 9: Trinity Sunday, General.

Rev. 19:6-7:

Hallelujah! The Lord our God is King;
  let us rejoice and give him glory.

A   1   Sing to the LORD a new song,
         for he has wrought a marvelous thing.
     With his right hand and holy arm,
         he himself has brought salvation.

    2   The LORD has made known his salvation,
         his righteousness open to the nations.
    3   He has remembered his love to Jacob,
         his faithfulness to the house of Israel.
 [3a]   All the ends of the earth have seen
         the salvation of our God.

B   4   Lift a jubilant shout to the LORD, O earth;
         rejoice and ring out his praises.
    5   Sing psalms to the LORD with the harp;
         with the harp and the melody of songs.
    6   With trumpets and the sound of the horn,
         shout with joy before the King, the LORD.
    7   Let the sea resound and everything in it;
         the world and all who dwell therein.
    8   Let the rivers clap their hands,
         and the hills sing together for joy.

C   9   Before the LORD who comes to judge the earth.
     He will judge the earth with justice,
     and the peoples with equity.

ANTIPHONS

Verse 3cd: Christmas.

Verse 2: Epiphany.

Ps. 96:11, 13:
Let the heavens rejoice and the earth be glad,
   before the LORD when he comes.

Matt. 1:23, 21:
His name will be called Emmanuel, "God with us,"
   for he will save his people from their sins.

Luke 2:10:
Behold, I bring you good news of great joy,
   which is come for all people.

Psalm 100

1   Shout for joy to the LORD, all the earth;
      serve the LORD with gladness,
      come before him with singing.

2   Know that the LORD—he is God;
      he made us, we belong to him,
      his people, the sheep of his pasture.

3   Enter his gates with thanksgiving;
      go into his courts with praise,
      give him thanks, bless his Name.

4   For the LORD is good;
      his merciful love is for ever,
      his faithfulness from age to age.

ANTIPHONS
Each verse is suitable.
Verse 3 with a Hallelujah: Thanksgiving Day, General.

A 1   Lord, hear my prayer,
      and let my cry come before you.

2   Do not hide your face from me
      in the day of my trouble.

[2a]   Incline your ear to me;
      when I call make haste to answer me.

3   For my days vanish like smoke;
      my bones burn like coals in the hearth.

4   My heart is smitten like withered grass,
      and I forget to eat my food.

5   Because of my constant groaning,
      I am but skin and bones.

6   I am like a vulture of the desert,
      and an owl among the ruins.

7   I lie awake and moan,
      as a lonely bird on a roof.

8   All day long my enemies taunt me;
      they deride me, using my name as a curse.

9   Ashes are the bread I eat;
      tears are mingled with my drink,

10   Because in your anger and wrath
      you picked me up, then threw me away.

11   My days are a lengthening shadow,
      and I wither away like grass.

B 12   You, O Lord, abide for ever;
      your Name endures from age to age.

13   You will arise and have pity on Zion;
      the time appointed has come to favor her.

14   Your servants love her stones even in rubble,
      and pity her in her dust.

15   The nations will revere your Name, O Lord,
      and all the kings of the earth your glory.

16   For the Lord will rebuild Zion,
      where his glory shall appear.

17   Then he will heed the plea of the destitute,
      and will not despise their prayer.

18   Let this be written for generations to come,
      that people yet unborn may praise the Lord:

19   "The LORD looked down from his sanctuary on high;
        from the heavens he beheld the earth,

20   That he might hear the groans of the prisoners,
        and set free those who were condemned to die."

28   The descendants of your servants will dwell secure,
        and their offspring be established in your sight,

21   That they may proclaim in Zion the Name of the LORD,
        and his praise in Jerusalem,

22   When the peoples are gathered together,
        and the kingdoms to serve the LORD.

C 23   He has broken my strength before my time,
        and has cut short the number of my days.

24   I said, "O my God, take me not away in the midst of my
        days,
        for your years endure through all generations.

25   From of old you laid the foundations of the earth,
        and the heavens are the work of your hands.

26   They shall perish, but you will endure;
        they will all wear out as a garment.

[26a]   You will change them like clothing,
        and they will pass away.

27   But you are always the same,
        and your years will never end."

ANTIPHONS

Verses 1 or 2: Lent, Holy Week.

Verses 12 or 27: General.

A 1 Bless the LORD, O my soul;
     with all my being, bless his holy Name!

2 Bless the LORD, O my soul,
     and forget not all his benefits.

3 He forgives all your sins,
     and heals all your diseases.

4 He redeems your life from the grave,
     and crowns you with mercy and loving-kindness.

5 He fills all your years with good,
     and renews your youth like an eagle's.

B 6 The LORD gives righteous judgments,
     and justice for all who are oppressed.

7 He made known his ways to Moses,
     and his deeds to the children of Israel.

8 The LORD is merciful and compassionate,
     slow to anger and rich in loving-kindness.

9 He will not always scold us,
     nor will he keep his anger for ever.

10 He has not treated or punished us,
     as our sins and misdeeds deserve.

11 As high as the heavens are above the earth,
     so great is his mercy to those who revere him.

12 As far as the east is from the west,
     so far has he removed our sins from us.

13 As a father has compassion for his children,
     so the LORD has compassion for those who revere him.

14 For he knows of what we are made;
     he remembers that we are but dust.

15 As for us, our days are like the grass,
     and like a wild flower in blossom.

16 When the wind blows over it, it is gone,
     and the place of it is known no more.

17 The love of the LORD for those who revere him
     endures for ever and ever.

18 His righteousness extends to their descendants,
     who keep his covenant and obey his commandments.

19 The LORD has fixed his throne in heaven,
     and his kingdom rules over all.

C 20 Bless the LORD, you angels of his,
his mighty ones who do his bidding,
and obey the voice of his word.
21 Bless the LORD, you heavenly armies,
his servants who do his will.
22 Bless the LORD, all his works,
in all places of his dominion.

Bless the LORD, O my soul!

ANTIPHONS

Verses 1, 2, 6, 8, 19, or 22: General.

1 John 4:16:

We know and believe the love God has for us;
whoever abides in love, abides in God.

1   Bless the Lord, O my soul!

A   O Lord, my God, how supreme is your greatness;
    you are clothed with majesty and glory.

2   You robe yourself with a mantle of light,
    and stretch out the heavens like a curtain.

3   You lay the beams of your dwelling on the waters,
    and make the clouds your chariot,
    to ride on the wings of the wind.

4   You make the winds your messengers;
    your servants are flames of fire.

B 5   You have set the earth on its foundations,
    so that it shall never move at any time.

6   You covered it with the ocean as a cloak,
    whose waters stood higher than the mountains.

7   At your command the waters turned back;
    at the voice of your thunder they fled.

8   From the mountains they flowed down to the valleys,
    to the places you appointed for them.

9   You set limits which they should not pass,
    so that they never again cover the earth.

C 10   You make springs that stream into the valleys,
    and run among the hills.

11   They give water for all the beasts of the field;
    in them the wild asses quench their thirst.

12   Beside them the birds of the air make their nests,
    and sing among the branches.

13   From your dwelling you water the mountains;
    the earth is filled with the fruit of your works.

D 14   You make the grass grow for the cattle,
    and plants for the use of man;
    That he may bring forth food from the earth,

15   and wine to gladden the heart;
    Oil to give a cheerful countenance,
    and bread to make us strong.

16   The trees of the Lord are full of sap,
    the cedars of Lebanon which he planted.

17 In them the birds build their nests;
    in their tops the storks make their home.
18 The high mountains are a refuge for the wild goats,
    and the rocks shelter the badgers.

E 19 You made the moon to mark the seasons;
    and the sun knows the time of its setting.
20 You make the darkness, and it is night,
    in which all the beasts of the forest prowl.
21 The young lions roar for their prey,
    seeking their food from God.
22 When the sun rises they steal away,
    to lie down and rest in their dens.
23 Man goes forth to his work
    and to his labor until the evening.

F 24 How manifold are your works, O Lord!
    In wisdom you have made them all;
    the earth is full of your creatures.
25 And there is the sea, vast and wide,
    with its swarms of living things without number,
    creatures both great and small.
26 They move there like ships;
    and there is Leviathan whom you made to play with.
27 All of them look to you
    to give them their food in due season.
28 When you give it to them, they gather it;
    when you open your hand, they are filled with good.
29 When you hide your face, they are troubled;
    when you take away their breath,
    they die and return to the dust.
30 When you send forth your Spirit, they are created,
    and you renew the face of the earth.

G 31 The glory of the Lord is everlasting;
    the Lord rejoices in his works.
32 If he looks at the earth, it trembles;
    if he touches the mountains, they smoke.

33 I will sing to the Lord as long as I live;
    I will praise my God as long as I breathe.

34   May my meditation please him;
         I will rejoice in the LORD.
35   Let sinners vanish from the earth,
         and let the wicked be no more.

         Bless the LORD, O my soul!
         Hallelujah!

ANTIPHONS

The psalm has its own antiphon.

Verse 1: Trinity Sunday, General.

Verse 30: Pentecost.

Hallelujah!

A 1 Give thanks to the LORD for he is good;
his merciful love endures for ever.

2 So let the redeemed of the LORD proclaim,
those whom he rescued from the enemy's hand,

3 Those whom he gathered out of the lands,
from east and west, from north and south.

B 4 Some wandered through desert wastes,
finding no way to a settled city.

5 They became hungry and thirsty;
their spirit was almost spent.

6 Then they cried to the LORD in their trouble,
and he delivered them from their distress.

7 He set their course on a straight way,
to a city where they might dwell.

8 Let them give thanks to the LORD for his mercy,
and the wonders that he did for them.

9 For he satisfies those who are thirsty,
and fills the hungry with good fare.

C 10 Some lived in darkness and gloom,
bound in misery with iron fetters.

11 For they rebelled against the words of God,
and spurned the counsel of the Most High.

12 He humbled their spirit with hard labor;
when they fell, there was none to help.

13 Then they cried to the LORD in their trouble,
and he delivered them from their distress.

14 He brought them out of darkness and gloom,
and broke asunder their bonds.

15 Let them give thanks to the LORD for his mercy,
and the wonders that he did for them.

16 For he shatters the gates of bronze,
and breaks the bars of iron in two.

D 17 Some were sick because of sinful ways;
their iniquities made them miserable.

18 They loathed any kind of food,
    and were very near to death's door.

19 Then they cried to the LORD in their trouble,
    and he delivered them from their distress.
20 He sent forth his word and healed them,
    and rescued them from the grave.

21 Let them give thanks to the LORD for his mercy,
    and the wonders that he did for them.
22 Let them offer sacrifices of thanksgiving,
    and declare his works with joyful acclaim.

E 23 Some went down to the sea in ships,
    to ply their trade in deep waters.
24 They saw the works of the LORD
    and his wonders in the deep.
25 With his voice he sent a gale,
    that tossed high above them the waves,
26 Lifted to the sky, then down in the deep;
    their spirit was dismayed and troubled.
27 They reeled and staggered like drunkards,
    and were at their wit's end.

28 Then they cried to the LORD in their trouble,
    and he delivered them from their distress.
29 He stilled the storm to a whisper,
    until the waves of the sea were quiet.
30 He brought them, glad at the calm,
    to the harbor where they were bound.

31 Let them give thanks to the LORD for his mercy,
    and the wonders that he did for them.
32 Let them extol him in the assembly of the people,
    and praise him in the council of the elders.

F 33 The LORD changed rivers to a desert,
    and water-springs to an arid land,
34 A fertile ground into a salt marsh,
    because the people who dwelt there were wicked.

35 Again, he turned deserts to pools of water,
    and arid ground to flowing springs,

36 Where he gave the hungry a home,
   to build a city to dwell in.

37 They sowed fields and planted vineyards,
   that yielded a fruitful harvest.

38 He blessed them, so that they multiplied;
   nor did he let their herds decrease.

39 When they were diminished and humbled
   by oppression, adversity and sorrow,

40 He poured his contempt on their rulers,
   and made them wander in trackless wastes.

41 Yet he raised the needy from affliction,
   and increased their families like a flock.

42 The righteous shall see this and rejoice,
   and the mouth of the wicked will be shut.

43 Whoever is wise will give heed,
   and consider the loving-kindness of the LORD.

ANTIPHONS

Verse 1: General.

The refrain of verses 6, 13, 19, 28.

Verse 43: (Strophe F).

A   1   The LORD said to my Lord:
"Sit at my right hand,
    until I make your enemies your footstool.

    2   The LORD send from Zion
    your sceptre to rule among your foes.

    3   Princely might was yours
    from the day of your birth in shining raiment.

[3a]   Like dew from the morning,
    from the womb I have begotten you."

B   4   The LORD has sworn; he will not recant:
"You are a priest for ever,
    after the order of Melchizedek."

    5   The LORD at your right hand
    will smite kings in the day of his anger.

    6   He judges the nations,
    smashes their heads, heaps their corpses far and wide.

    7   You will drink from a wayside brook,
    in victory hold your head high.

ANTIPHONS

Verse [3a]: Christmas.

Verse 4: Ascension.

Ps. 103:19:
The LORD has set his throne in heaven,
    and his kingdom rules over all.

Matt. 28:20:
Lo, I am with you always,
    even to the end of the world.

Hallelujah!

1 Blessed are they who fear the LORD,
and have great delight in his commandments.

2 Their offspring will be powerful in the land,
and their children who are upright will be blest.

3 In their house are wealth and riches;
their righteousness stands firm for ever.

4 Light shines in darkness for the upright,
for they are merciful and kind.

5 It is good for them to be generous in lending,
and to manage their affairs with justice.

6 Never will the righteous be perturbed;
and they will always be remembered.

7 They will not fear any news that is evil;
their heart is fixed, for they trust in the LORD.

8 Without any fear their heart is confident;
they will see the downfall of their enemies.

9 With open hand they give to the poor;
their righteousness stands firm for ever;
they will hold up their head with honor.

10 The wicked see it and are filled with anger;
they grind their teeth, then fade away,
for their hopes have come to nothing.

ANTIPHONS
Verses 1 or 4 with or without Hallelujah: Saints' Days, General

Hallelujah!

A 1 Praise the LORD, you servants of his;
Praise the Name of the LORD.

2 Blessed be the Name of the LORD,
now and for evermore.

3 From the rising of the sun to its setting,
let the Name of the LORD be praised.

B 4 The LORD is high above all nations,
and his glory is above the heavens.

5 Who is like the LORD our God,
seated enthroned on high?

6 Yet he humbles himself to behold
the heavens and the earth.

C 7 He takes up the weak from the dust,
and lifts the poor out of the trash-heap,

8 To seat them in the company of princes,
with the princes of his people.

9 He gives the childless woman a home,
as a happy mother of children.

ANTIPHONS
Verse 3: Easter, General.
Verse 9: Feasts of the Incarnation or of St. Mary.

Hallelujah!

A 1 When Israel came out of Egypt,
        and Jacob's house from people of strange speech,
    2 Judah became his sanctuary,
        and Israel his domain.

    3 The sea beheld it and fled,
        Jordan turned itself back.
    4 The mountains skipped like rams,
        and the little hills like lambs.

B 5 What caused you to flee, O sea?
        O Jordan, why did you turn back?
    6 You mountains, why did you skip like rams,
        and you little hills like lambs?

    7 Tremble, O earth, at the presence of the LORD,
        at the presence of the God of Jacob,
    8 Who turned the hard rock into a pool of water,
        and the flint-stone to a flowing fountain.

ANTIPHONS
Hallelujah! (Easter)

Preface

A 1   Give thanks to the LORD for he is good;
        his loving-kindness endures for ever.

2   Let the household of Israel now say:
    "His loving-kindness endures for ever."

3   Let the household of Aaron now say:
    "His loving-kindness endures for ever."

4   Let all who revere the LORD now say:
    "His loving-kindness endures for ever."

I

B 5   I called out to the LORD in my plight;
        he answered me and came to my rescue.

6   The LORD is on my side, I shall not fear;
    what can man do to me?

7   The LORD is on my side, he is my helper;
    I shall see my victory over my enemies.

8   It is better to take refuge in the LORD,
    than to put any trust in man.

9   It is better to take refuge in the LORD,
    than to put any trust in princes.

C 10   All the heathen peoples surround me;
        in the Name of the LORD I shall repel them.

11   They surround me, they surround me on every side;
    in the Name of the LORD I shall repel them.

12   They surround me like bees, like fire in brushwood;
    in the Name of the LORD I shall repel them.

13   I was very hard pressed and almost fell;
    but the LORD came to my rescue.

14   The LORD is my strength and my song;
    he has become my salvation.

15   Hear the shouts of joy and victory
    in the tents of the righteous:

    "The right hand of the LORD has triumphed!

16   The right hand of the LORD is exalted!
    The right hand of the LORD is victorious!"

17   I shall not die but live,
        to declare the deeds of the LORD.

18   He has given me a sore punishment,
        but he has not handed me over to death.

II

D 19   Open to me the gates of victory,
        that I may enter and give thanks to the LORD.

20   "This is the gate of the LORD;
           the righteous may enter it."

21   I thank you because you answered me;
        and you have become my salvation.

22   "The stone that the builders rejected
           has become the chief cornerstone."

23   This is the LORD's doing;
        it is marvelous in our sight.

24   "This is the day when the LORD has acted;
           let us rejoice and be glad in it!

25   Hosanna! Hosanna!
        Save us, LORD, and prosper us, we pray.

26   "Blessed is he who comes in the Name of the LORD;
           we bless you from the house of the LORD."

27   The LORD is God; his light shines upon us;
        form the procession with branches up to the altar.

28   "You are my God and I will praise you!
           You are my God and I will exalt you!"

29   Give thanks to the LORD for he is good;
        his loving-kindness endures for ever.

ANTIPHONS

Verses 1 and 29: General.

Verse 17: Easter season.

Verse 24: Easter Day.

Verses 25a and 26a: Palm Sunday.

[Parts V, XIV, XXI]

V

33 Teach me, O Lord, the way of your statutes,
and I shall always follow it.
34 Give me understanding that I may keep your law,
and observe it with my whole heart.
35 Lead me in the path of your commandments,
for that is my delight.
36 Incline my heart to your decrees,
and not to unjust gain.
37 Turn my eyes from looking at vanities,
and give me life in your way.
38 Fulfill your promise to your servant,
which you give to those who revere you.
39 Turn away the reproach which I fear,
for your judgments are good.
40 How I long for your precepts,
for in your righteousness you give me life.

XIV

105 Your word is a lantern to my feet,
and a light upon my path.
106 I have sworn and am determined
to keep your righteous judgments.
107 I am grievously afflicted;
revive me, O Lord, by your word.
108 Accept, O Lord, the willing offering of my lips,
and teach me your judgments.
109 Though I put my life always in my hand,
yet I do not forget your law.
110 The wicked have set a trap for me,
but I do not stray from your precepts.
111 Your decrees are my heritage for ever,
and the joy of my heart.
112 I apply my heart to fulfill your statutes
for ever, and to the end.

XXI

161   Princes of power oppress me;
          but my heart has awe in your word.
162   My delight is in your sayings,
          where I find abundant spoils.
163   I hate lies and detest them;
          your law is my love.
164   Seven times a day I praise you,
          because of your righteous judgments.
165   Great peace have they who love your law;
          nothing makes them stumble.
166   I hope for your salvation, O LORD,
          for I fulfill your commandments.
167   In my life I keep your decrees,
          and I love them beyond measure.
168   I have kept your precepts and decrees;
          and all my ways are before you.

ANTIPHONS

Many verses of the psalm are appropriate.

Ps. 1:2:
Their delight is in the law of the LORD;
    and in his law they meditate day and night.

1   I will lift my eyes to the hills:
     "Whence comes my help?"

2   My help comes from the LORD,
     the Maker of heaven and earth.

3   He will not let your foot slip;
     your Keeper will not sleep.

4   He who keeps watch over Israel
     never slumbers nor sleeps.

5   The LORD watches over you as a shade,
     over you and beside you,

6   So that the sun shall not hurt you in the day,
     nor the moon in the night.

7   The LORD will defend you from all evil,
     and keep you in safety.

8   The LORD watches over your going out and coming in,
     now and for evermore.

ANTIPHONS

Verse 7: General.

Rom. 15:13:
May the God of hope fill you
   with all joy and peace in believing.

A   1   I rejoiced when they said to me,
          "Let us go to the house of the Lord."
    2   Now at last we are standing
          within your gates, O Jerusalem.

B   3   Jerusalem is built as a city
          bound firmly together in unity.
    4   There the tribes go up,
          the tribes of the Lord—
[4a]   As he decreed for Israel—
          to praise the Name of the Lord.
    5   There are the seats of justice,
          the thrones of the house of David.

C   6   Pray for the peace of Jerusalem:
          "Prosperity to those who love you!
    7   Peace within your ramparts!
          Safety behind your towers!"
    8   For love of my brothers and friends
          I say, "Peace be with you!"
    9   For love of the house of the Lord our God,
          I will seek to do you good.

ANTIPHONS

Verses 1 or 3: General.

Gal. 4:26:
The Jerusalem which is above is free,
   and she is the mother of us all.

A 1   Blest is every one who reveres the LORD,
         and follows in his ways.

    2   From the rewards of your labor you will eat
         and be happy and prosper.

    3   Your wife will be a fruitful vine in your house,
         your children as olive-shoots about your table.

    4   Thus shall the one be blest
         who reveres the LORD.

B 5   The LORD bless you from Zion:
         "All the days of your life,
         May you see Jerusalem prosper,

    6   And behold your children's children."
         Peace be upon Israel!

ANTIPHONS

Verse 1: Marriage, General.

Psalm 130

1   Out of the depths have I called to you, LORD.
        LORD, hear my voice.

2   O let your ear be attentive
        to the voice of my plea.

3   LORD, if you take account of our sins,
        who then can stand?

4   But with you there is forgiveness,
        that you may be worshipped.

5   I wait, I wait for the LORD;
        in his word is my hope.

6   I wait for the LORD more than the watchers
        who look for the dawn.

7   O Israel, look for the LORD's mercy and love,
        for his bounteous redemption.

8   For he will set Israel free
        from all his sins.

ANTIPHONS

Verses 3-4: Ash Wednesday.

Verses 7-8: Holy Week.

Verses 5-6: Burial.

I

A 1 Remember David, O LORD,
    and all his troubles,
  2 The oath that he swore to the LORD,
    his vow to the Mighty One of Jacob:
  3 "I will not enter into my house,
    nor climb into my bed;
  4 I will not allow my eyes to sleep,
    nor my eyelids to slumber,
  5 Until I find a place for the LORD,
    a dwelling for the Mighty One of Jacob."

B 6 We heard of the Ark in Ephratah,
    and found it in the fields of Jearim.
  7 Let us go up to his dwelling place;
    let us worship before his footstool.
  8 "Arise, O LORD, go up to your resting place,
    and with the Ark of your strength!
  9 Let your priests be robed with righteousness,
    and your faithful people shout for joy.
 10 For the sake of your servant David,
    turn not away from your Anointed."

II

C 11 The LORD has sworn an oath to David;
    his word he will never break;
    "A descendent of your line
    I will set on your throne.
 12 If your sons keep my covenant,
    and the laws that I teach them,
    Their sons shall for ever
    sit upon your throne."
 13 For the LORD has chosen Zion,
    and desired her for his home.

D 14 "This is my resting place for ever;
    here will I dwell, as I have chosen.
 15 I will bless her with abundant riches,
    and satisfy her poor with bread.

16	I will robe her priests with salvation; her faithful people will shout for joy.
17	I will make the house of David flourish, and light a lamp for my Anointed.
18	His enemies I will clothe with shame; but his crown will shine and blossom."

ANTIPHONS

Verse 11: Advent.

Ps. 89:36-37:
His throne shall endure as long as the sun,
and shall stand fast for ever as the moon.

Isa. 9:7:
His Name will be called Wonderful, Counsellor,
and Prince of Peace;
The increase of his rule shall have no end,
upon David's throne for evermore.

Jer. 33:15:
I will raise up for David a righteous Branch,
who will do justice and righteousness in the land.

Mark 11:9-10:
Hosanna! Blessed is he who comes in the Name of the Lord;
blessed is the kingdom of our father David. Hosanna!

A   1   With my whole heart I will thank you, O Lord;
        before the gods I will sing your praise.
     2   I will bow down and worship at your holy temple,
        and praise your Name for your faithfulness and love.
     3   Your Name and your word are exalted above all things;
        yet when I called, you answered and strengthened me.

B   4   All the kings of the earth will praise you, O Lord,
        when they have heard the words of your mouth.
     5   They will sing of the ways of the Lord,
        how great is the glory of the Lord.
     6   For though the Lord is high, he has regard for the lowly;
        as for the proud, he considers them from afar.

C   7   Though I walk in the midst of trouble, you save me;
        against the fury of my foes, you stretch out your hand.
     8   With your right hand you deliver me;
        the Lord will fulfill his purpose for me.
  [8a]   Your loving-kindness, O Lord, endures for ever;
        do not forsake the work of your hands.

ANTIPHONS

Any verse as appropriate.
Verse 4: Epiphany season.

A 1   O LORD, you have searched me,
    and know me thoroughly.

  2   You know whether I sit down or stand up;
    you can discern my thought from afar.

  3   You watch where I walk and lie down,
    and are familiar with all my ways.

  4   There is not a word on my lips,
    but you, LORD, know it already.

  5   You surround me behind and before;
    your hand is ever laid upon me.

  6   Such knowledge is too wonderful for me,
    so high that I cannot reach it.

B 7   Where shall I escape from your Spirit?
    where can I flee from your presence?

  8   If I climb up to heaven, you are there;
    you are there, if my bed be in the underworld.

  9   If I take wing to the dawning sun,
    or dwell at the limits of the sea,

 10   Even there will your hand lead me,
    and your right hand will hold on to me.

 11   If I say, "Surely the darkness will hide me,
    and the night will cover me round about,"

 12   Yet darkness is not dark to you,
    for the night is as bright as the day;
    darkness and light to you are both alike.

C 13   You have created my inmost being,
    and formed me in my mother's womb.

 14   I praise you in awe for making me;
    your work is wondrous, and I know it well.

 15   My body was not hidden from you
    when moulded secretly in the depths.

 16   In your book you wrote of me unformed,
    and of my deeds that should come to pass.

 17   How unsearchable are your thoughts, O God!
    how without limit is the sum of them!

 18   To count them would be more than the grains of sand;
    were I to finish, you would still be there.

D 23   Search me, O God, and know my heart;
         test me and know my thoughts.
24   Watch lest I walk in any evil way,
         and lead me in the way everlasting.

ANTIPHONS

Verse 23: General.

Acts 17:27-28:
He is not far from each one of us;
    in him we live and move and have our being.

1   I will exalt you, O God my King,
    and bless your Name for ever and ever.

2   Day after day will I bless you,
    and praise your Name for ever and ever.

A   3   Great is the LORD and worthy of great praise;
        there is no limit to his greatness.

4   Age to age praises your works,
    and proclaims your mighty deeds.

5   They ponder the splendor and glory of your majesty,
    and all your marvelous wonders.

6   They will relate your awesome acts,
    and recount your greatness.

7   They will call to remembrance your great goodness,
    and sing out with joy your righteousness.

B   8   The LORD is gracious and merciful,
        slow to anger and steadfast in love.

9   The LORD is good to every one;
    his compassion reaches all whom he has made.

10 All your creation praises you, O LORD;
    all your faithful people bless you.

11 They proclaim the glory of your kingdom,
    and tell of all your power;

12 That every one may know of your might,
    and the glorious splendor of your kingdom.

C   13 Your kingdom is an everlasting one
        that endures throughout all ages.

[13a] The LORD is faithful in all his words,
       and gracious in all his deeds.

14 The LORD upholds all who have fallen,
    and raises up those who are bowed down.

15 The eyes of all creatures look to you,
    and you give them their food in due time.

16 You open your hand wide,
    and satisfy the want of all living things.

D   17 The LORD is just in all his ways,
        and gracious in all his deeds.

18 The LORD is near to all who call to him,
　　to all who call to him sincerely.
19 He fulfills the desires of those who revere him;
　　he hears their cry and saves them.
20 The LORD preserves all those who love him;
　　but those who are wicked he destroys.
21 My mouth will speak the praise of the LORD;
　　let every creature bless his holy Name for ever.

ANTIPHONS

Verses 1-2, or any other verse, as appropriate.
Blessed be the LORD
　and blessed be his Name
　for ever and ever (the Qumran Psalm scroll).

1   Hallelujah!
        Praise the LORD, O my soul!

2   I will praise the LORD all my days;
        I will sing to my God while I live.

3   Put not your trust in princes,
        nor in man, in whom is no help.

4   When they breathe their last, they return to the earth;
        their plans perish on that very day.

5   Happy are they whose help is the God of Jacob,
        whose hope is in the LORD their God,

6   Who made the heaven and the earth,
        the sea, and all that is in them.

7   He keeps his promise for ever;
        he renders justice to the oppressed.

[7a]   He gives bread to the hungry;
        the LORD sets the prisoners free.

8   The LORD opens the eyes of the blind;
        the LORD lifts up those who are bowed low.

9   The LORD cares for the strangers,
        and supports the widow and orphan.

[9a]   The LORD loves the righteous;
        but he thwarts the way of the wicked.

10   The LORD shall reign for ever;
        your God, O Zion, for all generations.

        Hallelujah!

ANTIPHONS
Hallelujah: General.
Verse 10: Epiphany.

Hallelujah!

A 1 How good to make melody to our God;
how pleasant to honor him with praise!

2 The LORD rebuilds Jerusalem,
and gathers the exiles of Israel.
3 He heals the broken-hearted,
and binds up all their wounds.
4 He numbers all the stars,
and calls each one by its name.
5 Our LORD is great and mighty;
his wisdom is without measure.
6 The LORD lifts up the lowly,
but casts the wicked to the ground.

[Hallelujah!]

B 7 Sing to the LORD and give him thanks;
make melody to our God with the harp!

8 He veils the heavens with clouds,
and provides rain for the earth.
[8a] He clothes the hill-sides with grass,
and with green plants for our needs,
9 With fodder for the cattle,
and food for the calling ravens.
10 The strength of a horse or a man
is not what pleases the LORD;
11 But his delight is in those who revere him,
and who hope in his gracious love.

[Hallelujah!]

C 12 Praise the LORD, O Jerusalem!
O Zion, praise your God!

13 He makes strong the bars of your gates,
and blesses your children within you.
14 He establishes peace in your borders,
and satisfies you with the finest wheat.

15 He sends out his command to the earth,
and his word runs very swiftly.

16   He showers the snow, white as wool,
         and scatters the hoar-frost like ashes.

17   He sprinkles the ice like bread-crumbs,
         and the cold becomes unbearable;
18   Then he utters his word, the ice thaws;
         his wind blows and the waters flow.

19   To Jacob he makes known his word,
         his statutes and judgments to Israel.
20   He has not done this for any other nation,
         nor revealed to them his decrees.

Hallelujah!

ANTIPHONS

Each strophe has its own antiphon in verses 1, 7, and 12, respectively, with Hallelujah at beginning and end, and also, if desired, at the end of strophes A and B.

Verse 5: General.

Verses 8 or 14: Thanksgiving Day.

102

Hallelujah!

A 1 Praise the Lord from the heavens;
　　　praise him in the heights.

2 Praise him, all you angels;
　　　praise him, all his host.

3 Praise him, sun and moon;
　　　praise him, all you stars of light.

4 Praise him, highest heavens,
　　　and you waters above the heavens.

5 Let them all praise the Name of the Lord,
　　　for at his command they were created;

6 He made them fast for ever and ever,
　　　with a law they shall never breach.

B 7 Praise the Lord from the earth:
　　　sea-monsters and all deeps;

8 Fire and hail, snow and fog,
　　　storm-wind, obeying his word;

9 Mountains and all hills,
　　　fruit-trees and all cedars;

10 Wild animals and all cattle,
　　　reptiles and winged birds;

11 Kings of the earth and all peoples,
　　　princes and all rulers of the world;

12 Young men and maidens,
　　　elders and children together.

13 Let them all praise the Name of the Lord,
　　　for his Name alone is exalted;
　　　his majesty is above earth and heaven.

14 He has raised up strength for his people;
　　　he is the praise of all his faithful ones,
　　　Israel's children, a people near to him.

Hallelujah!

ANTIPHONS

The Hallelujah after each verse or group of verses.

Gen. 1:31: God saw that all he had made was very good.

Prov. 3:19: The Lord by wisdom founded the earth,
　　　by understanding he established the heavens.

Hallelujah!

1 Praise God in his holy place.
　　Praise him in the heaven of his power.

2 Praise him for his mighty deeds.
　　Praise him for his excelling greatness.

3 Praise him with blast of the horn.
　　Praise him with harp and lyre.

4 Praise him with drum and dance.
　　Praise him with strings and pipe.

5 Praise him with resounding cymbals.
　　Praise him with clashing cymbals.

6 Let everything with breath
　　Praise the LORD.

Hallelujah!

ANTIPHONS

The Hallelujah is the basic antiphon, to which verse 6
　may be added.

A. A TABLE OF LITURGICAL USE

Any of the psalms in this collection are suitable for use at the Holy Eucharist on Sundays or other times of special observance, when appropriate to the lessons or themes of the day. The following list consists of psalms traditionally assigned to certain days or seasons of the Christian year, or associated with special occasions of worship.

Day or Season	*Psalms*
ADVENT	24, 25, 50, 80, 85, 132
CHRISTMAS	19 (Part I), 89, 98, 110
EPIPHANY	2, 19, 72, 138, 146
LENT	25, 27, 34, 51, 91, 102, 130
HOLY WEEK	22, 27, 31, 42-43, 57, 69, 102
EASTER	2, 23, 33, 66, 114, 118
ASCENSION DAY	24, 47, 110
PENTECOST	29, 48, 104
TRINITY SUNDAY	8, 19 (Part I), 96
SAINTS' DAYS	1, 15, 24 (Part I), 34, 112
ROGATION DAYS AND THANKSGIVING DAY	65, 67, 100, 104, 145, 147

Special Occasions	
BAPTISM	23, 42
MARRIAGE	128
BURIAL	23, 27, 90, 121, 130
DAILY PRAYERS	
Morning	19, 95, 103, 148
Noon	33, 91, 113, 119
Evening	23, 27, 90, 139
SUNDAYS	84, 96, 100, 122
HOLY COMMUNION	
Before	34:1-10, 43, 65:1-5, 84
After	145, 148, 150

B. NOTES ON LITURGICAL USE

1. General or Saints' Days.
Antiphonally by verses or by strophes. If by strophes, verse 3 may be in unison.

2. Easter, Epiphany, or Transfiguration.
Antiphonally by verses or by strophes. A soloist may take the narrative portions and a chorus the quoted statements; or a second soloist may take the quoted statements in strophes B and C. Or, a chorus may take the narrative portions and soloists the quoted statements.

8. Christmas, Holy Innocents, Trinity Sunday, or General.
Verses 1 and 10 in unison; verses 2-9 antiphonally by verses or by strophes.

15. General or Saints' Days.
In unison or antiphonally by verses. A soloist may take verse 1, with antiphonal responses by the lines in verses 2-5, and unison in verse 6.

19. Christmas, Epiphany, Feasts of Apostles (Part I); Saints' Days (Part II); Trinity Sunday and General (Parts I and II).
Parts I and II may be used separately or together, antiphonally or by strophes. In Part II verses 10 and 14 should be in unison.

22. Holy Week; General (Part II).
Parts I and II may be used separately or together, antiphonally by verses or by the groups of verses within the strophes. Verses 11 and 19 (omitting verses 20-21) may be in unison. If the psalm is shortened, strophes B and D may be omitted.

23. Easter, General, Baptism, Burial.
In unison or antiphonally by verses. The shift from third to second person also suggests an antiphonal rendering by strophes; or a cantor may take strophe A, and strophe B may be used as a choral response.

24. Advent, Ascension, General.
Antiphonally by verses. In Part I, verses 1-2 and 6 may be in unison, with soloists taking alternately verses 3 and 4-5. In Part II, a soloist may take the questions in verses 8a and 10a, with the rest sung in unison.

25. Advent, Lent, General.
Antiphonally by verses, or by pairs of verses from verse 2 through verse 21, with verses 1 and 22 in unison.

27. Lent, Holy Week, Burial, General.
Antiphonally by verses or by strophes, with verses 6 and 14 in unison. The two Parts may be sung together or separately. A good effect is achieved when Part II is sung before Part I.

29. Pentecost.
Antiphonally by verses with refrains in unison; or strophes A and C in unison, with soloists taking verses of strophe B and the full chorus the refrains.

31. Holy Week, General, especially strophes A and D.
Antiphonally by verses, with verses 6-8 and 17-18 omitted, if desired. At the Eucharist, the four strophes may be used successively for introit, gradual, offertory, and Communion.

33. Easter, General.
Antiphonally by verses or pairs of verses, with verses 1 and 22 in unison.

34. Lent, Saints' Days, General.
Antiphonally by verses or pairs of verses. Either strophe may be sung independently.

36. General.
Antiphonally by verses or pairs of verses.

42-43. Holy Week, Baptism (Psalm 42), Eucharist (Psalm 43), General.
Antiphonally by verses with the refrain in unison; or a soloist may sing the strophes, with the chorus taking the refrain. The two psalms may be used separately.

46. Advent, General.
Antiphonally by verses or by strophes, with the refrain in chorus.

47. Ascension, General.
Antiphonally by verses, or each strophe by antiphonal chorus.

48. Pentecost, General.
Antiphonally by verses; or a soloist may take the strophes, with chorus at verses 3, 8, and 14.

50. Advent, General.
Antiphonally by verses or pairs of verses. Soloists may sing verses 5, 7, 16a, and 21cd-23; but verse 23 may be in unison. Strophe C may always be omitted.

51. Ash Wednesday, other occasions of penitence.
Antiphonally by verses or pairs of verses. Verses 18-19 may be omitted.

57. Holy Week, General (strophe C).
In strophes A and B, the verses antiphonally; in strophe C verses 5 and 11 in unison, verses 7-10 antiphonally.

65. Rogation Days, Thanksgiving Day, General.
Antiphonally by verses, with verse 1 in unison.

66. Easter, General.
Antiphonally by verses, with verses 12c and 20, if desired, in unison. Strophe D may be omitted. At the Eucharist: A as an introit; B and C as a gradual; D as an offertory; and E as a Communion.

67. Thanksgiving Day, General.
Antiphonally by verses, with the refrain of verses 3, 5, and [7a] in unison.

69. Holy Week.
The first verse in unison; the rest of the psalm antiphonally by verses or pairs of verses. Strophes A and C, and B and D may be sung as independent psalms.

72. Epiphany.
Antiphonally by verses or pairs of verses. Verses 18-19 may be sung in unison as a doxology, or they may be omitted.

80. Advent.
Antiphonally by verses or by strophes, with the refrain in unison. Strophe A, as an invocation, may also be sung as a chorus.

84. General.
Antiphonally by verses; but verses 1, 4, 5, 8, 9, and 12 may be sung in unison, with the intervening verses sung antiphonally or by selected soloists.

85. Advent, General.
Antiphonally by verses, with verse 7 in unison—also repeated after verse 13, if desired.

89. Advent, Christmas (Preface, Parts I and II), General (Part I).
Antiphonally by verses or pairs of verses. Verse 52 may be omitted. Verses 1-2 and 3-4 by soloists, if desired.

90. New Year's, Burial, General.
Antiphonally by verses: Part II may be omitted, if desired.

91. First Sunday in Lent; General (as appropriate).
Antiphonally by verses, pairs of verses, or strophes. Strophe D may be sung in unison.

95. General.
Verses 1-2 and 4-5 may be sung antiphonally, with verses 3 and 6-7 as refrains. Strophe C may be omitted, or sung as a separate psalm if appropriate. The last line of verse 7 may be used with either portion. If strophe C is used alone, verse 7d may be sung by a soloist and verses 8-11 sung antiphonally or in unison.

96. Trinity Sunday, General.
Antiphonally by verses, or by strophes with strophe E in unison.

98. Christmas, General.
Antiphonally by verses or by strophes with strophe C in unison.

100. General.
It should be used as an introit or invitatory. Antiphonally by verses or in unison. A soloist may sing the first line of each verse, and the two following lines may be sung in unison.

102. Lent or Holy Week, General (strophe B).
Antiphonally by verses or groups of verses.

108

103. General.

Antiphonally by verses. Any strophe may be used independently or in combination.

104. Pentecost, General.

Antiphonally by verses or by strophes. Verse 35 may be omitted.

107. General.

Antiphonally by verses or by groups of verses. A soloist may take verses 4-5, 10-12, 17-18, and 23-27, with the other verses antiphonally or in unison. Strophe F may be used as a separate psalm, or omitted if desired.

110. Christmas, Ascension.

Antiphonally by verses; or a soloist may take verses 1 and 4, with the other verses in unison. The two strophes may be used independently.

112. Saints' Days, General.

Antiphonally by verses. Verse 10 may be omitted.

113. Feasts of the Incarnation or of St. Mary, Easter, General.

In unison; or verse 1 in unison, the other verses antiphonally.

114. Easter.

Antiphonally by verses or by strophes.

118. Palm Sunday, Easter.

Antiphonally by verses, with verses 1 and 29 in unison. A more dramatic effect as follows:
  A: Verses 2-4, a soloist takes the first half verse, a chorus the second half verse.
  ⎰B: A soloist or small chorus takes verses 5-7, 10-15*ab*,
  ⎱C: 17-18; full chorus sings verses 8-9 and 15*c*-16.
  D: Antiphonally; or a soloist takes the odd-numbered verses, full chorus the even-numbered verses and verse 29.
Because of the length of the psalm, the strophes may be distributed through the service: A at introit; B-C at gradual; verses 19-24 at offertory; verses 25-29 at Communion.

119. General.

Antiphonally by verses; or each part separately in unison.

121. Burial, General.

In unison or antiphonally by verses.

122. General.

In unison or antiphonally by verses. Strophe A may be sung by soloists, with strophes B and C antiphonally.

128. Marriage, General.

In unison or antiphonally by verses.

130. Holy Week, or days of penitence, Burial.
Antiphonally by verses or by pairs of verses.

132. Advent, Christmas (Part II).
Antiphonally by verses or by strophes. The verses in quotation marks may be sung by soloists.

138. Epiphany, General.
Antiphonally by verses or by strophes.

139. General.
Antiphonally by verses or by pairs of verses.

145. Thanksgiving Day, General.
Antiphonally by verses, or by strophes with verses 1-2 as refrain. Any strophe may be omitted without loss of the sense.

146. Epiphany, General.
Antiphonally by verses or by pairs of verses, with verses 1-2 in unison.

147. Rogation Days, Thanksgiving Day, General.
Antiphonally by verses, with verses 1, 7, and 12 in unison. The Hallelujah may be inserted after strophes A and B. Each strophe may be used separately or in combination.

148. General.
Antiphonally by verses, with verses 5-6 and 13-14 in unison.

150. General.
In unison or antiphonally by verses, with the Hallelujah after each verse if desired.

C. NOTES ON THE PSALMS

1. The first Psalm is a preface which the final editors of the Psalter considered an appropriate thematic introduction. It opens with a beatitude, a literary form beginning with "Blessed" that is common in the Bible, most notably in our Lord's Beatitudes.[1] It refers to a person whose character is praiseworthy and who is fortunate in the sight of God.

The theme of the psalm is the contrast of the two ways of just and wicked people and their respective rewards in God's judgments upon them now and at the end of time. In the Bible the word *way* refers to a style of life, the direction and goal of one's devotion and behavior. Among the Jews the way of God consisted in constant study of the law, God's revealed instruction, and the application of it to one's manner of life. Our Lord himself, in a context recalling this psalm, spoke of a wide and easy way that leads to destruction, and a narrow and hard way that leads to life.[2] He taught "the way of God truthfully," and was himself "the way, and the truth, and the life." [3] In the book of Acts a common name for the early Christians was simply "the Way." [4]

The figure of the tree in verse 3 is cited from Jeremiah 17:8. Both John the Baptist and our Lord contrasted good and bad trees and their respective fruits.[5] There are also overtones here of the "tree of life" planted by rivers of water in God's paradise.[6]

[1] Matthew 5:3-11; Luke 6:20-22.
[2] Matthew 7:13-14.
[3] Matthew 22:16; John 14:6; see James 1:25; 2 Peter 2:2, 15, 21.
[4] 9:2, 19:9, 23, 22:4, 24:14; cf. 16:17, 18:26.
[5] Matthew 3:10; Luke 3:9; Matthew 7:17-20, 12:33; Luke 6:43-44.
[6] Genesis 2:8-10; Revelation 22:1-2.

2. The second Psalm, like the first, has no title, and was probably added also as a preface by the final editors of the Psalter, with an appended pious reflection to verse 12: "Blessed are all they who take refuge in him." Taken together, the two psalms point to the dominant religious concerns of late Judaism: devotion to the law, and expectation of a messianic deliverer from foreign oppression.

It is one of the "royal psalms" that celebrates the accession or anniversary of a Hebrew king. It is arranged in four strophes, each with a different speaker: A, the plot of the kings and rulers; B, God's answer from heaven; C, the decree of the appointment and destiny of God's Son; and D, the advice of the psalmist to the rulers.

Despite its bellicose imagery, the early Christians used the psalm as a prophecy of Jesus "the Anointed" [Hebrew, *Messiah;* Greek, *Christos*]. Strophe A referred to the plots of Herod Antipas and Pontius Pilate against Jesus, and to the persecution of his disciples.[1] Verse 7 in strophe C was variously understood as a prophecy of his birth or baptism,[2] his resurrection and heavenly enthronement,[3] or his eternal begetting as the Son of God before all ages.[4]

The translation of verse 11b, difficult in the Hebrew, follows an emendation favored by many scholars.

[1] Acts 4:23-30.
[2] Luke 1:35, 3:22.
[3] Acts 13:33; Romans 1:3-4.
[4] Hebrews 1:5.

111

8. This hymn belongs among the creation songs of the Psalter (see 19:1-6, 104, and 148). It recalls in verse 3 an ancient myth of God's victory in creation over the resistant forces of chaos.[1] But the principal interest of the psalm is in man, created in the image of God and given dominion over all other creatures.[2]

"Son of man" in verse 5 is simply a Hebrew synonym for "man." The ancient rabbis and early Christian writers took the phrase as a reference to the messianic Son of man, though the context does not support this interpretation. In verse 6, the Hebrew text reads "little less than God," and in the Greek version, "little lower than the angels." The author of Hebrews made much of the latter as a prophecy of Christ's dominion.[3] The gospel of Matthew used verse 2, again in the Greek version, as a prophecy of our Lord's triumphal entry into Jerusalem; but in the church's liturgy it has been associated with the feast of the Holy Innocents on December 28.[4]

> [1] Genesis 1:2; Psalm 89:9-11.
> [2] Genesis 1:26-28; see Job 7:17.
> [3] Hebrews 2:5-9.
> [4] Matthew 21:16; see also 2:16-18.

15. The psalm is not a poem, but an instruction in the form of question and answer, with a concluding promise of blessing. It is sometimes known as the Ten Commandments Psalm, from the 10 precepts listed in verses 2–5 for those who would be acceptable to God in worship and in daily life. Based on the two chief commandments of love to God and to our neighbor,[1] these precepts should not be understood as a legal code of self-righteous morality, but in the spirit of our Lord's teaching that right actions spring from right attitudes.

> [1] Matthew 22:36-40; Mark 12:28-33; Luke 10:25-28.

19. Psalm 19 is a combination of two poems of independent date and emphasis. Together they recount God's revelation in the natural order of creation and in his historical law. The first poem is an ancient hymn that has parallels with an old Babylonian hymn to the sun-god Shamash, though there is no suggestion in the psalm that the Hebrews considered the sun and stars to be divine. The second poem recounts in strophe C God's gift of the law, and in strophe D the psalmist prays for grace to keep it. Each of the last two strophes concludes with a reflective comment.

St. Paul quoted verse 4 with reference to the spread of the gospel throughout the world.[1] The early church fathers related verses 5–6 to the prophecy of Malachi of the coming of "the sun of righteousness," [2] and associated these verses with New Testament images of Christ as Sun [3] and Bridegroom.[4] Hence the psalm came to be appointed in the liturgy for feasts of the incarnation and of the saints. The psalm has also influenced the Sanctus of the liturgy [5] by the addition of "heaven" to the line: "Heaven and earth are full of your glory."

> [1] Romans 10:18.
> [2] Malachi 4:2.
> [3] Luke 1:78; Revelation 1:16, 21:23.
> [4] Mark 2:19-20; John 3:29; Ephesians 5:32; Revelation 19:7, 21:2.
> [5] Isaiah 6:3.

22. Psalm 22 has left an indelible place in Christian devotion because of its prophetic use by the Gospel writers in their accounts of our Lord's crucifixion. Verses 1, 7–8, and 16–17 cannot be read without recalling Jesus' agony on

the cross. Yet it is important to remember that when Jesus uttered his cry (verse 1), he was citing a psalm that ends in a song of victory.

The psalm consists of two complementary poems. The first is a lament of one in acute suffering and imminent danger of death, a poignant and realistic portrayal in detail of bodily anguish and sensations of fear. But the suffering reaches deeper in a spiritual dread of being deserted by God. There is no wrestling, however, with the meaning of his affliction, as in the Book of Job, or any probing of the redemptive character of suffering, as in the Servant Songs of Isaiah. On the other hand, the thanksgiving hymns of the second part have a universal scope that reaches beyond the present deliverance to encompass the dead and generations yet to be born. The first part is intensely personal; the second is communal and liturgical.

There are many textual obscurities in the verses of the second part. The translation follows emendations generally accepted by scholars. Verse 25 has been transposed as a more likely transition to the hymns that follow.

23. A favorite image among the Hebrews, who were a pastoral people, was that of the faithful shepherd who feeds, guides, and protects his flock. He symbolized God's care for his people and the oversight of their rulers and priests as God's representatives, such as David, the shepherd boy whom God chose to be king.[1] The prophets used the image both for God and for his Messiah in the age to come.[2]

Our Lord used the figure in his parable of the lost sheep [3] and in his teaching about himself as the Good Shepherd.[4] No simile of his ministry was more apt than the remark of his compassion for the multitudes because they were "like sheep without a shepherd." [5] His lowly birth in a manger was first announced to shepherds in the field; [6] and his last commission to Peter after his resurrection was "to feed his sheep." [7]

The earliest pictorial portrayal of our Lord in Christian art was as the Good Shepherd—a picture associated with Baptism, hence the use of this psalm during the Easter season when Baptisms were usually administered.[8]

[1] 1 Samuel 16.
[2] Isaiah 40:11; Jeremiah 23:1-4, 31:10; Ezekiel 34:1-16.
[3] Matthew 18:12-13; Luke 15:3-7.
[4] John 10:1-16.
[5] Matthew 9:36; Mark 6:34.
[6] Luke 2:8.
[7] John 21:15-17.
[8] See 1 Peter 2:25, 5:4; Hebrews 13:20.

24. The psalm is another combination of two poems of independent date and purpose. Part II is the older psalm, sometimes associated with David's bringing the ark of the Lord to Jerusalem.[1] The "heads" are the gate towers, which symbolize the Lord's council who receive him as a conqueror. The reference to the "everlasting doors," however, suggests a procession into the temple gates of the sanctuary, built after David's time. Part I is similar to Psalm 15, and notes the ethical qualifications for those who would be acceptable worshipers in the temple services.

At an early time Christians associated Psalm 24 with our Lord's ascension. Later, when the season of Advent was instituted, it was applied also to his entering our humanity in his incarnation. The "King of glory" is revealed both in his coming into the world and in his return to the Father in heaven.

[1] 2 Samuel 6:12-15.

25. Psalm 25 follows an acrostic pattern, a form common in the Psalter and other poems of the Old Testament.[1] Each verse begins with a letter of the Hebrew alphabet in succession. In this psalm, verse 1 lacks a parallel line—it was probably like verse 21b; and the last verse is an editorial addition. Catchwords form inner links to the verses, such as "put to shame, teach, way," etc. Despite these restrictions of form, the psalm has a depth of sincerity, and its maxims provide sound spiritual guidance. Though cast in the form of a prayer, its content is more closely akin to the wisdom literature.

[1] Other acrostic psalms in this collection are 34, 112, 119, and 145.

27. Two psalms of contrasting mood were joined to form Psalm 27. The first one is a song of confidence in God's unfailing support in the face of foes, and of assurance in his protection of those who find refuge in his worship. It has the tone of a victorious leader in battle who has returned to give sacrifices of thanksgiving in the temple. The second poem is a deeply personal lament addressed to God for deliverance from false accusers. Yet it also ends in hope and in trust to see "the goodness of the LORD" (verse 13).

The early Christian fathers interpreted the psalm with reference to the Christian's faith in God in the midst of temptations and persecutions. The LORD of the psalm was generally taken to be Christ, in whose suffering and victory the Christian found hope. Hence the psalm was traditionally appointed in the Lenten season.

29. This psalm is one of the oldest and most dramatic poems in the Bible. It depicts God's voice speaking in a thunderstorm that arises in the Mediterranean Sea, then passes over the Lebanon mountains and on to the south over the desert wilderness. An opening anthem glorifies this manifestation in the courts of heaven; a closing anthem does the same for the worshipers in the temple.

The association of Israel's God with thunder and lightning is an ancient one, and reverberates often in the Old Testament.[1] It sounds again in the New Testament; and the seven voices of God in the psalm are reflected in the seven thunders of the Apocalypse.[2] In Jewish worship the psalm was sung on the eighth and last day of the feast of Tabernacles and also at the feast of Pentecost. The latter feast was associated with the giving of the law on Mount Sinai; and this use of the psalm was adopted by the church for its own Pentecost festival, recalling "the rush of a mighty wind" and "tongues of fire." [3]

The refrains after verses 2, 4, 6, and 9 are composed from verses 3b, 7, and 9b of the psalm.

[1] Exodus 9:22-23, 19:16-19, 20:18; 1 Samuel 7:10, 12:17-18; 1 Kings 19:11-12; Job 26:14, 37:4-5, 40:9; Psalms 77:18, 104:7; Isaiah 29:6.
[2] John 12:29; Revelation 10:3-4.
[3] Acts 2:1-5.

31. The psalm is one of contrasts. At its heart is the lament of one in dire straits, who is shunned by his friends while his foes plot against his life. This is followed by a prayer of trust in God's deliverance. Songs of trust preface and conclude the psalm—in the latter the psalmist summons others who have known his experience, to share in his hope and trust. In the Christian liturgy the psalm has often been assigned to Holy Week, as a fitting expression of Christ's own experience in his passion.

33. This is a hymn of praise to God for what he is in himself, for his creation,

114

his lordship over the nations, and his care for Israel. Though not an acrostic psalm, such as Psalms 25 and 34, its 22 verses may have been suggested by that form, which follows the 22 letters of the Hebrew alphabet. Because of verse 19, the psalm has been associated, in the church's liturgy, with the Easter season.

34. Psalm 34 is an acrostic poem (see note on Psalm 25); each verse begins with a letter of the Hebrew alphabet. But the verse corresponding to the letter *Waw* has dropped out after verse 5, and an additional verse, possibly editorial, has been added at the end to make up for the missing letter. The psalm is an instruction framed in praise, for those who would live according to God's ways and worship.

36. The verses of this psalm included here are a hymn of thanksgiving for God's love, which was set in a contrasting frame concerned with the way of the wicked. In the New Testament verse 9 is reflected in John 1:4, 9.

42-43. The two psalms form a unity from their common theme and refrain. The psalmist is an exile among heathen foes, somewhere in the north of Palestine in the region of Mount Hermon. He looks with longing upon his former role in the worship of God at Mount Zion. Yet he holds to his hope and trust that God will bring him again to share in the festivals and worship of his own people. In the Hebrew text of verse 6 the reading is "hill of Mizar," an unknown location. In this translation we have followed the reading of the Septuagint, "little hill," which in the context could refer to Mount Zion.

In the Christian liturgy the psalms have had a prominent place. Psalm 42 was sung in procession to the font for the Easter Baptisms—the deer panting "for the water-brooks," symbolizing those seeking the baptismal waters. Psalm 43 was related to the Eucharist, as a favored preparation for those seeking the joy of Communion with God at his altar.

46. Psalm 46 is a vision of the world now and in the end time. It contrasts the secure, sovereign might of God in his heaven with the tumults of nature and nations on earth. The imagery was taken up into the Jewish and early Christian apocalyptic visions.[1] Those whose refuge is in God are secure in his help whatever may be a crisis or terror.

The refrain of verses 7 and 11 is inserted after verse 3, where the Hebrew text has a *selah*, a rubric that refers either to an instrumental interlude or a praise-shout.

[1] Matthew 24; Mark 13; Luke 21; for verse 5, see Revelation 22:1-2.

47. The psalm reflects the teaching of Isaiah about God's universal kingship over the whole world. Its ceremonies may also reflect the acclamations that accompanied the enthronement of a Hebrew king.[1] In Jewish worship it was appointed for the New Year's festival at the time of the harvest; in the church's liturgy it has been associated with the feast of our Lord's Ascension.

The horn in verse 5 is the *shofar*, a ram's horn sounded at festivals (f. 98:6, 150:3).

[1] 1 Kings 1:38-40; 2 Kings 9:13, 11:12.

48. This is one of the Songs of Zion, sung by pilgrims to the city and temple of Jerusalem.[1] Other examples in this collection are Psalms 84 and 122. There are many similarities to Psalm 46, though this psalm is less apocalyptic. The "ships of Tarshish" (verse 7) are often mentioned in the Old Testament, but the location is uncertain. In some contexts it appears to be a Phoenician colony

in the Mediterranean, possibly Tartessus in Spain. But other contexts (see Psalm 72:10) point southward to Arabia and the Indian Ocean.

[1] Isaiah 26:1-2; Jeremiah 31:23; for a Christian counterpart, see Hebrews 12:22-24; Revelation 21:2-4.

50. The scene is a grand assize when God comes to judge his people before heaven and earth. Strophe A is a summons, with an accompaniment of storm that recalls Psalm 29. Strophe B is more of an instruction than a judgment and reflects the teaching of the prophets, especially Isa. 1:10-17. Strophe C is a stringent judgment upon the wicked. Verse 7d has been added to complete the sense and the verse parallelism. In the church's liturgy the psalm is used in Advent with its recurring theme of the final judgment of Christ.

51. No other passage of the Old Testament equals this psalm for its depth of understanding of personal estrangement from God and of restoration to communion with him by one who has been forgiven. The Hebrew title of the psalm designates it as "A Psalm of David, when Nathan the prophet came to him, after he had gone in to Bathsheba." [1] The psalm may well have been inspired by that event, but it reflects more nearly the teaching of the prophets.[2] Many scholars consider verses 18–19 to be a later editorial addition to connect the very personal view of verses 16–17 to the cult. If they are an original part of the psalm, then the date is certainly no earlier than the exile.

The psalm is associated with penitential occasions, and in the church with the liturgy of Ash Wednesday. In the daily services of the monks it was employed for a similar purpose as a confession of sin every day at Lauds. In the Eastern churches it is recited daily at Matins.

[1] 2 Samuel 12.
[2] Isaiah 57:15, 63:7–64:12; Jeremiah 31:31-33; Ezekiel 11:19, 36:26.

57. Two psalms of contrasting character have been conjoined in Psalm 57. Strophe C has also been repeated in Psalm 108:1-5. The first psalm, strophes A and B, describes the sufferings of one who has been laid low yet has never lost his faith in God's power and goodness in saving him. The second, strophe C, is a thanksgiving for God's answer in rescuing the afflicted one. The psalm finds a place in the church's liturgy of Holy Week, looking to God's praise when Christ "awakes the dawn" (verse 8c).

In the Hebrew text the pause of selah is noted after verses 3 and 5; hence verse 6 is probably erroneously inserted after verse 4. Its transposition to a place as an antiphon to strophe C is adopted in many modern versions.

65. Psalm 65 is a song of harvest festival, centered in the temple in Jerusalem. Strophe A sets the ground for thanksgiving: God's forgiveness, blessings, providence, and power, both among his people and among those at the far reaches of the earth and the sea. Strophe B is the hymn celebrating the rich harvests in grain and flocks that have followed abundant rains. In the liturgy the psalm is favored for Rogation Days and Thanksgiving Day.

66. This is a song of victory, similar to Psalm 118. A leader of the people has gone through a hard struggle with his foes, but by God's help he has come out alive and victorious. He then comes with rich offerings to the temple, with hymns of thanksgiving shared with all the people. Strophe A is a gathering hymn of praise; strophes B and C recount the victor's story, with reference to the Exodus of God's people. Strophe D accompanies a procession to the altar

116

for sacrifices, and strophe E is a concluding hymn of praise. In the church's liturgy the psalm is appointed for the Easter season.

67. The psalm is correlative with Psalm 65, as a thanksgiving for an abundant harvest. God's goodness to his people is occasion to summon his universal praise by all peoples and nations. In this version the refrain has been added after the third strophe.

69. Psalm 69 is one of the longest laments in the Psalter. Strophe A is the lament proper: the psalmist is under attack from the lies of his enemies and is laid very low, without any support from friends or relatives. Strophes B and C are his prayer for God's deliverance. A following strophe, omitted in this version as unsuitable for Christian worship, is a bitter malediction upon the psalmist's enemies. Strophe D is the thanksgiving for deliverance associated with the similar fortunes of Israel.

The psalm is often reflected in the Gospel narratives, and especially in the accounts of the Lord's passion. Hence in the liturgy it has been associated with Holy Week.

72. This hymn in honor of the coronation of a Hebrew king is one of two psalms attributed to Solomon. (The other, not in this collection, is 127.) In the form of a prayer, it celebrates the ideals of the people for their king: justice, prosperity, peace, and recognition by other rulers and nations. Emphasis is given to the king's concern for and defense of the poor. The boundaries of his rule are ideally extended from the Mediterranean Sea to the Euphrates River.[1] Verses 18–19 are not an original part of the psalm, but are a doxology added by the editors to conclude the second book of the Psalter.

Later Judaism interpreted Psalm 72 in a messianic sense, and so did the early church. It became the proper psalm for the Epiphany festival—the reference in verses 10–11 being applied to the visit of the Magi to the infant Jesus.[2]

[1] Verse 8; see Psalm 80:11.
[2] Matthew 2:1 ff.

80. The lament of the psalmist has to do with a disaster to God's people. The Greek title of the psalm refers to the Assyrians; and this, with the names in verses 1–2, suggests that the psalm reflects the fall of the Northern Kingdom to the Assyrians in 721 B.C.[1] The figure of Israel as a vine or vineyard is frequent in the Old Testament.[2] In the New Testament it is applied to Christ and his church.[3] For this reason Christians took verses 17–18 as a prophecy of the coming of Christ, and so associated the psalm with the season of Advent.

The repeated refrain in the psalm occurs in slightly different wording in the Hebrew text. In this version it has been conformed throughout to the text of verse 19.

[1] 2 Kings 17:1-18.
[2] Isaiah 5:1-7, 27:2-4; Jeremiah 2:21; Ezekiel 15 and 17:5-6; Hosea 10:1.
[3] Mark 12:1-9; John 15:1-6.

84. This is a pilgrim Song of Zion (see note on Psalm 48). The joy of the psalmist in worship in the temple has a counterpoint in the unfilled longing for such joy in Psalms 42–43. In verses 1 and 12 God is addressed as *Yahweh Sabaoth* ("LORD of hosts," as in Isaiah 6:3 and the Sanctus of the liturgy). In Christian usage the reference in verse 9 was transferred to Christ, the

Anointed King; and God's house in verse 10 to the church, which is the temple of the Holy Spirit.

85. The psalm was composed in a time of distress for the people, though an exact occasion cannot be identified. The first strophe is a lament that includes both a remembrance of God's past favors and a cry for speedy deliverance from the present circumstances. The second strophe is a prophecy of hope that God's favor will return and the land will be fruitful and at peace. The psalm is assigned to the liturgy of Advent, looking toward Christmas, the coming of the Prince of Peace.

89. Psalm 89 combines a hymn, an oracle, and a lament. It centers on God's promise to David and his descendants, and the grievous fall of his house when the Babylonians captured Jerusalem and King Jehoiachin in 597 B.C. and King Zedekiah in 587 B.C.[1] Since the dynasty of David was not permanent, the church understood the psalm as a prophecy of Christ, whose kingdom is everlasting, and who, as a descendant of David, fulfilled the promise. It has customarily been associated with Advent and Christmas.

The psalm has a preface—two antiphons that give its major themes: God's everlasting love and faithfulness, and his oath to David about his dynasty. Part I is a hymn of praise based on the first theme. It is a creation song, with many primitive notes, such as God's rule over other gods and his conflict with the dragon of the deep (Rahab) in his creation of the world. Part II recalls the story of God's choice of David as king.[2] Part III describes vividly the disgrace of the dynasty in the fall of Jerusalem, with Part IV as a lament for the disaster.

[1] 2 Kings 23:31—25:30; Jeremiah 36-39.

[2] 2 Samuel 7:8-17.

90. The Hebrew title of Psalm 90 calls it "A Prayer of Moses, the man of God"; but its first part is more in the manner of a reflective piece of wisdom. With vivid imagery it contrasts man's mortality, transitory existence, and sinfulness with God's eternity and righteousness.[1] The second part is possibly a second psalm. The interest shifts from man's universal condition to a prayer for Israel's deliverance from affliction. In late New Testament writings [2] and some of the early church fathers, verse 4 was taken symbolically, if not literally of the millennial reign of Christ before the final judgment.

In Jewish liturgy the psalm was appointed for the Sabbath, the day that signified God's eternal rest from his creation. In Christian usage it has been favored for services at New Year's and at funerals—marking the end of one time and the beginning of a new time.

[1] For verse 3, see Genesis 3:19; for verses 4-5, see Job 14:1-2; Psalm 103:15-16; Isaiah 40:6-8.

[2] See 2 Peter 3:8; Revelation 20:1-7.

91. The ancient world believed in demonic spirits who were responsible for all sorts of evil that befall the unwary. The root of this psalm, according to many scholars, was in magic spells against demons bringing sudden sickness and death. But the psalmist has turned this fear into a magnificent hymn of trust in God's providence over those who make him their refuge. His power of protection is reinforced by the use of four names of the deity: *Elyon, Shaddai, Yahweh,* and *Elohim,* translated in the first two verses as "Most High," "Al-

mighty," "LORD," and "God." There are many reminiscences in the psalm of the Song of Moses.[1] The last strophe is a liturgical response to the first three.

Verses 11–12 were quoted by Satan in his temptation of Jesus.[2] This explains the assignment of the psalm in the liturgy of the First Sunday in Lent, when the Gospel account of our Lord's temptation is read. In the Daily Offices of the Eastern church the psalm is appointed for the noonday service of Sext; in the Western churches, at the service of Compline.

[1] Deuteronomy 32.

[2] Matthew 4:5-6; Luke 4:9-11.

95. The psalm is one of the temple hymns that celebrates God's kingship over nature and his people. From ancient times the church has used it as an invitation to worship in the first service of each day.

It is probable that strophe C was originally independent of strophes A and B. But the skillful linking of the two, through the warning of verse 7d gives it a unity in contrast. The image of God as "the Rock" of salvation in verse 1 is recalled in verses 8–9. In their trek through the desert the Israelites became thirsty and began to grumble and find fault with God for their distress. So at God's command, Moses struck the rock at Horeb, and water gushed out from it—hence the names he gave the place: Meribah ("Dispute") and Massah ("Testing").[1] St. Paul saw the incident as a warning for our instruction. The "rock was really Christ" and the water from it "the supernatural drink" which Christ gives us.[2]

Verse 11 refers to God's punishment of the people for their unfaithfulness, so that most of them did not finally enter the land of Canaan, the promised "place of rest."[3] The author of Hebrews interpreted the "rest" not as that of Canaan, but of a new "Today" for those who believe in Christ, whose "rest" will be in the age to come.[4]

[1] Exodus 17:1-7; Numbers 20:10-13.

[2] 1 Corinthians 10:1-11.

[3] Numbers 14:26-35; Joshua 5:6.

[4] Hebrews 3:7—4:11.

96. The psalm celebrates the universal kingship of Israel's God over all creation, including the peoples whose gods are but lifeless idols. There are similarities with Psalm 98 and with Isaiah.[1] A version of it is included in the account of David's bringing the Ark to Jerusalem, which omits, as in this version, verse 10c, "He will judge the peoples with equity" (cf. Psalm 98.9c).[2] In verse 9 the phrase "beauty of holiness" literally means "holy array," i.e., the attire appropriate to sacred ritual. The word "dance" translates a Hebrew word meaning "whirl, reel, or writhe." As a hymn of creation the psalm has been used in the church's liturgy on Trinity Sunday.

[1] Isaiah 42:10.

[2] 1 Chronicles 16:23-33.

98. Similar in phrase to Psalm 96 and Isaiah,[1] verse 6 suggests that in Jewish worship the psalm was used at the New Year's festival. In Christian liturgy it has been associated with Christmas. For though the emphasis in Psalm 96 is on creation, in this psalm it is basically a theme of God's salvation for his people. In this translation certain words and phrases have been derived from the ancient Greek version, which was the Bible of the early church.

[1] Isaiah 52:10.

100. The ancient title of the psalm calls it "A Psalm for the Thank-offering." It was probably sung in procession at such a sacrifice. It has been called a summary of the "creed of Judaism"—and so of Christianity: The Lord is God; he is our creator; we are his people; he is good; his loving-kindness is everlasting; his faithfulness endures for ever.

102. In this lament the psalmist is extremely ill and faces death, and his affliction is seen as being due to God's anger. Yet he gives himself in trust to God's abiding years without end; and support is given him by his faith in God's restoration of his people in exile and the rebuilding of Jerusalem, where all peoples will come to praise him. This close association of the affliction of the individual and of the people of God is characteristic of much of the Psalter; for the hope of each is intimately bound together. In the church's liturgy, Psalm 102, often classed as one of the seven penitential psalms (see Psalms 51 and 130), is appointed for Holy Week.

103. This psalm of praise for God's love echoes many passages of the Old Testament.[1] The figure of God as our "Father" in verse 13, so characteristic of Jesus' teaching, has some basis in other Old Testament passages.[2]

[1] Exodus 34:6-7, cf. verses 8-9; Isaiah 40:6-8, cf. verses 15-16.

[2] Deuteronomy 32:6; Isaiah 63:16, 64:8; Jeremiah 3:4, 19; Malachi 1:6, 2:10.

104. This hymn of creation is unique in the Psalter. Though it has parallels in ancient Near Eastern texts, its conception is thoroughly Hebraic. God's creation in all its manifestations is not only what he makes, but what he continually re-creates day by day. The psalmist calls his poem a meditation (verse 34), and he bases it, with some freedom, on the account of creation in Genesis 1–2.

It is difficult to make the uneven strophes exactly fit the days of creation in the Genesis story. The scheme followed here is: A, light and the elements; B, the earth and its formation; C, the waters; D, vegetation; E, sun and moon; F, the living creatures; G, praise. A scheme more like Genesis I would combine C and D, and divide F either before or after verse 27. The sea monster Leviathan of verse 26 possibly refers to a dragon common in Near Eastern creation myths; more popularly, it is a whale.

The church has associated the psalm with the feast of Pentecost because of verse 30, since the outpouring of the Spirit on Pentecost was the beginning of a new creation.

107. This psalm is a hymn of praise for God's care to those in special situations of distress: travelers in the desert, prisoners, the sick, and seafarers in stormy weather. It may have been used at thank offerings for deliverance (cf. verses 22, 32). Strophe F may be a later addition, for it paraphrases the other strophes and ends with a wise saying. Verse 40 may be a gloss from Job.[1]

[1] See Job 12:21a, 24b.

110. Like Psalm 2, this psalm was probably composed for a Hebrew king's accession or anniversary. Though ascribed to David, it has undergone successive revisions, so that in many places the text is obscure, especially in verse 3. In this translation the verse has been translated from the Greek version, since this has given it an important place in the church's prophetic understanding of the psalm. No other psalm is more often quoted in the New Testament.

The psalm consists of two oracles, each followed by prophetic comment.

In the first the Messiah is confirmed as Lord. Jesus used this as a prophecy of David about himself, in a controversy with the Jewish leaders.[1] The second oracle is prominent in the epistle to the Hebrews as a prophecy of our Lord's priesthood.[2]

In the church's liturgy the first oracle has been related to our Lord's incarnation (verse 3), and the second oracle to his ascension (verse 4).

[1] Matthew 22:44; Mark 12:36; Luke 20:42-43; cf. Acts 2:34-35; Hebrews 1:13, 10:12-13.
[2] Hebrews 5:6, 7:1-3, 15-21.

112. This is an acrostic psalm (see note on Psalm 25), in which each half verse begins in succession with a letter of the Hebrew alphabet. It is a companion piece to Psalm 111, also an acrostic, which celebrates the righteousness of God among his people. In this psalm the righteous who fear the LORD and keep his commandments are honored. The liturgy often appoints this psalm for saints' days, even though the good fortune of many saints is spiritual rather than material.

113. The group of Hallelujah psalms, 113–118, known as the Hallel or Egyptian Hallel (from Psalm 114:1) was sung by the Jews at their principal festivals. It is probable that Jesus sang these psalms with his disciples at the Last Supper.

Strophe C recalls the story and song of Hannah,[1] a childless woman whose prayers were answered by God in the gift of her son Samuel. Her song is reflected in Mary's Magnificat:

> He has cast down the mighty from their throne,
> and has lifted up the lowly.[2]

The figure of the childless woman who gives birth to more children than the married woman appears in Isaiah as a projection of Israel's revival after the exile, and is used by St. Paul as a prophecy of the church.[3]

The psalm has been used by the church on feasts of the Incarnation and of St. Mary, and, with other Hallel psalms, in the Easter season. Verse 3 has a parallel in the prophecy of Malachi,[4] which the early Christians saw fulfilled in the church's worship.

[1] 1 Samuel 2:8.
[2] Luke 1:52.
[3] Isaiah 54:1; Galatians 4:27.
[4] Malachi 1:11.

114. The second of the Hallel group of psalms (see above on Psalm 113) celebrates in short compass the redemptive events of Israel's exodus from Egypt across the Red Sea, to the crossing of the River Jordan into the promised land where later the temple ("sanctuary," verse 2) was built on Mount Zion. Two important incidents of the pilgrimage are also cited: the earthquake at Mount Sinai when God revealed his law (verse 7)[1] and the water which God supplied from the rock (verse 8).[2]

The early Christians transferred the use of the Hallel psalms to their own Easter celebration of Jesus' "exodus" [3] for the redemption of his people. The passages through the Red Sea and across the Jordan were types of baptism into the new covenant; the "water from the rock" was Christ's gift of life to us in our Baptism.[4]

[1] Exodus 19:16-19; cf. Judges 5:4-5.
[2] Exodus 17:1-6; Numbers 20:1-11.
[3] Cf. Luke 9:31.
[4] 1 Corinthians 10:1 ff.

118. Psalm 118 concludes the Hallel psalms (113-118) sung at the principal festivals. It is a liturgical hymn for a procession to the temple. In strophe A the praise-shouts of the several groups that form the procession resound. Strophes B and C accompany the march to the temple. A victory song of a warrior who has triumphed in hard-fought battle with his enemies (the *goyim,* "heathen") is interspersed with choral refrains. Strophe D consists of anti-phonal responses and praise-shouts at the gate and within the precincts of the temple.

Verse 27b is probably a rubric describing a ceremony used at the feast of Tabernacles, when the people cut willow and palm branches to carry in procession, and waved them about the altar as they sang their hosannas. The Psalter scroll from Qumran contains several verses of this psalm in a different order; and after verse 9 it has an additional line: "It is better to take refuge in the LORD than to trust in a thousand people." It also has a hallelujah shout at the end.

From early times the church has used this psalm at Easter. Verse 24 is the most ancient antiphon of Easter Day. The psalm is also associated with Palm Sunday because of the quotation of verses 25–26 in the Gospel accounts of our Lord's triumphal entry into Jerusalem. Verses 22–23 are appended to our Lord's parable of the wicked tenants in the vineyard.[1] The figure of Christ as the "cornerstone" of the new temple of his body, the church, is common in other New Testament writings.[2]

[1] Matthew 21:42; Mark 12:10; Luke 20:17.

[2] Acts 4:11; Ephesians 2:20; 1 Peter 2:4ff.

119. With its 176 verses this is the longest poem in the Psalter. It is a giant acrostic. Each of its 22 parts begins in succession with a letter of the Hebrew alphabet, and this letter begins each of the eight verses of the respective part. We have chosen here three characteristic parts, representing the letters *He, Nun,* and *Shin.*

To some the psalm is a poetic tour de force; others see it as a remarkable achievement of personal devotion. Given its restrictive structure and inevitable repetitions, the psalm has no less an extraordinary variety of expressions. It is at once a hymn, a meditation, and a prayer centered in devotion to God's Law (Torah) as applied to life. Seven synonyms for the Law recur constantly: *statutes, commandments, decrees, precepts, judgments, sayings, word;* and these are frequently interspersed with *way* and *path.*[1]

The psalm was probably not intended for liturgical use but rather for private meditation. In the Daily Offices that developed in the church, the psalm's several parts were distributed in the short daytime services of Prime, Terce, Sext, and Nones.

[1] Compare Psalm 19:7-12.

121. Psalms 120–134 form a collection within the Psalter, each of which bears the title translated "A Song of Degrees" or "A Song of Ascents." Three are ascribed to David and one to Solomon. It is generally thought that this collection was a devotional anthology for pilgrims going to Jerusalem. Psalm 121 is in any case a true pilgrimage song (see notes on Psalms 48 and 84). It recalls the dangers of the journey—a slip on a mountain climb, sunstroke and moonstroke, and other unforeseeable risks. But the song is of God's constant protection. He watches over each of his worshipers day after day as he does over Israel. It is thus a psalm of trust.

122. Psalm 122 is also a pilgrim song that expresses the joy of one who has at last reached Jerusalem and its temple. In strophe B the psalmist notes his admiration for the city. Verse 3b is variously understood to refer either to the compactness of the city's buildings or to the unity of those who live there or come to worship there. Strophe C is his prayer for this "city of peace" with words that play around the sound of the word for peace *(shalom)*. In the New Testament Jerusalem is the symbol of the city of God, the "new Jerusalem" prepared in heaven.[1]

[1] Galatians 4:25-26; Hebrews 12:22; Revelation 21.

128. The pilgrim of this psalm receives a blessing at the temple on Mount Zion for his family and for his labors in vineyard and olive grove. He is one who "reveres the LORD and walks in his ways." Traditionally it has been a favored psalm at the celebration of a marriage.

130. The inclusion of Psalm 130 in the pilgrim collection (Psalms 120–134) gives to the group an unusual spiritual depth. The pilgrim has a profound sense of his alienation from God because of his sins. Yet he "waits" patiently in full assurance that mercy will be given him. His confidence lies both in God's word (verse 5) and in his love for Israel (verse 8).

Commonly known by its Latin title *De profundis,* the psalm has been one of great comfort to believers in time of anguish and penitence, and in the hour of death. When applied to Christ, as the one who was "numbered with the transgressors" and "bore the sin of many," [1] the psalm has been used also in Holy Week.

[1] Isaiah 53:12; cf. John 1:29.

132. This psalm commemorates David's bringing the Ark of God from Kiriath-jearim to Mount Zion.[1] It reaffirms the promise of God to David and his descendants.[2] The psalm may have been used at the coronation of a king of Judah, a descendant of David. In verse 6 the place-name "Ephratah" is usually identified with Bethlehem, the city of David. Some scholars prefer to read "Ephraim," since Kiriath-jearim was near Shiloh.[3]

There are four equal strophes: A, David's vow to find a suitable temple for the Lord; B, a choral synopsis of the finding and bringing of the Ark, symbol of God's presence, to Jerusalem; C, God's oath to David and his descendants; and D, God's promise concerning his future blessings upon Mount Zion. Christian usage has associated the Anointed of David's line with Christ, the Messiah or "Anointed One." In the liturgy it has been traditionally assigned to the season of Advent.

[1] 1 Samuel 6:1-2, 20—7:2; 2 Samuel 6:1-15; 1 Chronicles 15:1-3, 25-29.
[2] 2 Samuel 7:11-16; cf. Isaiah 11:10.
[3] Cf. 1 Samuel 1:1, 9, 3:3.

138. This is a song of thanksgiving for God's help after a time of trouble from some unspecified enemy. It is offered in the temple; and the psalmist extends his praise to include "all the kings of the earth." The reference to "kings" in contrast with the "lowly" has made the psalm one of those appointed in the Epiphany season.

139. Many who love the Psalter consider Psalm 139 its finest poem. There is nothing in the Scriptures to match its intensely personal understanding of the all-pervading presence and knowledge of God. Yet there is no reflection of

the community and its worship. Verses 19–22, omitted here, may not be original to the psalm, for they are an outburst of imprecation and hatred of the wicked that seem out of place in what is otherwise a calm meditation. The closest parallel in the New Testament is the speech of St. Paul in Athens.[1]

[1] Acts 17:22-31; cf. Hebrews 4:12-13.

145. Psalm 145 is an acrostic (see note on Psalm 25). Each verse begins successively with a letter of the Hebrew alphabet. Most Hebrew manuscripts omit verse 13cd, for the letter *Nun*, but it is supplied here from the ancient Greek and Latin versions. It also is contained in the recently discovered scroll of the Psalter from Qumran. Much of the psalm is derived from other verses in the Psalter; yet it has its own power of expression. The dominant themes of the four strophes are in sequence: God's greatness, goodness, faithfulness, and justice. Verses 15-16 have been a favored blessing at meals.

146. This psalm is the first of a group of five Hallelujah Psalms that conclude the Psalter. They are sometimes called the Greek Hallel to distinguish them from the Egyptian Hallel (Psalms 113–118). All of them are liturgical hymns. There is little in Psalm 146 that is original. Many of its verses are borrowed from other psalms. But the total effect is strong, and its emphasis upon God's concern for the needy is noteworthy.[1] The first line of verse [9a] has been transposed from verse 8c. In Christian liturgy it is associated with the Epiphany season.

[1] Cf. Isaiah 61:1 ff.

147. In the ancient Greek version of the Psalter, Psalm 147 is divided into two psalms, verses 1-11 and 12-20, and attributed to the prophets Haggai and Zechariah. Verses 7-11 may be a third psalm, since each strophe begins with a new summons to praise. There are close affinities with Isaiah and the great hymn of Job.[1] In each strophe there is praise for God's creative providence and for his special favor to Israel, and particularly to the broken-hearted, the humble, and the devout ones who keep the law. There are echoes of the psalm in our Lord's Sermon on the Mount.[2] The psalm is often appointed for festivals of thanksgiving.

[1] Isaiah 40:26 (verse 4), 56:8 (verse 2), 61:1 (verse 3); Job 38:22-41.
[2] Matthew 6:25-33; Luke 12:23-31.

148. The psalm summons all creatures and all living beings in heaven and earth to praise the Lord, each sphere being divided by an appropriate refrain (verses 5-6 and 13-14). The order of creation generally follows the account of Genesis 1. A close parallel is the Song of the Three Children in the Old Testament Apocrypha. With Psalms 149 and 150 it has been sung in the daily morning Office of Lauds in the Eastern and Western churches; for the name *Lauds* comes from the opening Latin word of these psalms: *Laudate*, "Praise ye."

150. Each of the five books of the Psalter concludes with a doxology. In this collection we have noted them at the end of Psalms 72 and 89. Psalm 150 is the doxology both for the fifth book and for the entire Psalter. Verse 1 unites God's praise in his earthly and his heavenly sanctuaries. Verse 2 states the reason for this praise. Verses 3-5 call upon the players and their instruments in the temple orchestra to join in the joyful sound. Verse 6 includes every living being in the chorus of hallelujah.

D. THE CONSULTATION ON COMMON TEXTS

The Consultation on Common Texts was formed in March 1968 by representatives from the Inter-Lutheran Commission on Worship, the Commission on Worship of the Consultation on Church Union, and the International Committee on English in the Liturgy of the Roman Catholic Church. Its purpose was to study and develop contemporary English forms of liturgical texts that might be shared in common by churches engaged in ecumenical dialog and negotiation and in liturgical renewal.

Much of the preliminary work was taken up and refined by a larger body known as the International Consultation on English Texts (ICET), which has produced several editions of *Prayers We Have in Common*, the latest edition being that published in 1975 by the Fortress Press, Philadelphia. These texts have now been incorporated in authorized liturgies of many English-speaking churches throughout the world.

The work of the Consultation on Common Texts continues, however, in liturgical projects, such as this Psalter, which may be useful to the English-speaking churches of North America. Its members are drawn from the three bodies noted above and from other churches which may desire to be represented, including from time to time observers from the Orthodox church. The following churches are now represented in the Consultation:

The American Lutheran Church

The Christian Church (Disciples of Christ)

The Episcopal Church

The Lutheran Church in America

The Lutheran Church–Missouri Synod

The United Methodist Church

The Presbyterian Churches

The Roman Catholic Church

The United Church of Canada